Other titles include *Up & Running* with:

AutoSketch 3	*Norton Desktop for Windows*
Clipper 5.01	*Norton Utilities 6*
CompuServe	*Norton Utilities on the Macintosh*
CorelDRAW 2	*PageMaker 4 on the PC*
dBASE III PLUS	*PageMaker on the Macintosh*
DOS 3.3	*PROCOMM PLUS 2.0*
DOS 5	*Q & A 4*
Excel 3 for Windows	*Quattro Pro 3*
Flight Simulator	*Quicken 4*
Grammatik IV 2.0	*Windows 3.0*
Harvard Graphics 3	*Word for Windows*
Harvard Graphics for Windows	*Word for Windows, Version 2.0*
Lotus 1-2-3 Release 2.3	*WordPerfect 5.1*
Lotus 1-2-3 Release 3.1	*WordPerfect 5.1 for Windows*
Lotus 1-2-3 for Windows	*XTreeGold 2*
Mac Classic	
Mac System 7	

Computer users are not all alike. Neither are SYBEX books.

We know our customers have a variety of needs. They've told us so. And because we've listened, we've developed several distinct types of books to meet the needs of each of our customers. What are you looking for in computer help?

If you're looking for the basics, try the **ABC's** series, or for a more visual approach, select full-color **Teach Yourself** books.

Learn Fast! books are two books in one: a tutorial, to get you off to a fast start, followed by a command reference, to answer more advanced questions.

Mastering and **Understanding** titles offer you a step-by-step introduction, plus an in-depth examination of intermediate-level features, to use as you progress.

Our **Up & Running** series is designed for computer-literate consumers who want a no-nonsense overview of new programs. Just 20 basic lessons, and you're on your way.

SYBEX **Encyclopedias** and **Desktop References,** and **A to Z** books provide a comprehensive reference and explanation of all of the commands, features and functions of the subject software.

Sometimes a subject requires a special treatment that our standard series don't provide. So you'll find we have titles like **Advanced Techniques, Handbooks, Tips & Tricks**, and others that are specifically tailored to satisfy a unique need.

You'll find SYBEX publishes a variety of books on every popular software package. Looking for computer help? Help Yourself to SYBEX.

For a complete catalog of our publications:

SYBEX Inc.
2021 Challenger Drive, Alameda, CA 94501
Tel: (510) 523-8233/(800) 227-2346 Telex: 336311
Fax: (510) 523-2373

Up & Running with Windows 3.1

Up & Running with Windows™ 3.1

Joerg Schieb

SYBEX®

San Francisco • Paris • Düsseldorf • Soest

Acquisitions Editor: Dianne King
Series Editor: Joanne Cuthbertson
Translator: David J. Clark
Editor: Peter Weverka
Project Editor: Barbara Dahl
Technical Editors: Martin Moore
Word Processors: Ann Dunn and Susan Trybull
Book Designer: Elke Hermanowski
Icon Designer: Helen Bruno
Screen Graphics: Cuong Le
Desktop Production Artist: Helen Bruno
Proofreader: David Silva
Indexer: Ted Laux
Cover Designer: Archer Design

Screen reproductions produced with Collage Plus.
Collage Plus is a trademark of Inner Media Inc.

SYBEX is a registered trademark of SYBEX Inc.

TRADEMARKS: SYBEX has attempted throughout this book to distinguish
proprietary trademarks from descriptive terms by following the capitalization
style used by the manufacturer.

SYBEX is not affiliated with any manufacturer.

Every effort has been made to supply complete and accurate information.
However, SYBEX assumes no responsibility for its use, nor for any infringe-
ment of the intellectual property rights of third parties which would result
from such use.

Authorized translation from German Language Edition.
Original copyright © SYBEX-Verlag GmbH 1992.
Translation copyright © SYBEX Inc. 1992.

Library of Congress Card Number: 92-81039
ISBN: 0-89588-843-2

Manufactured in the United States of America
10 9 8 7 6 5 4 3 2 1

SYBEX
Up & Running Books

The Up & Running series of books from SYBEX has been developed for committed, eager PC users who would like to become familiar with a wide variety of programs and operations as quickly as possible. We assume that you are comfortable with your PC and that you know the basic functions of word processing, spreadsheets, and database management. With this background, Up & Running books will show you in 20 steps what particular products can do and how to use them.

Up & Running books are designed to save you time and money. First, you can avoid purchase mistakes by previewing products before you buy them—exploring their features, strengths, and limitations. Second, once you decide to purchase a product, you can learn its basics quickly by following the 20 steps—even if you are a beginner.

The first step usually covers software installation in relation to hardware requirements. You'll learn whether the program can operate with your available hardware as well as various methods for starting the program. The second step often introduces the program's user interface. The remaining 18 steps demonstrate the program's basic functions, using examples and short descriptions.

A clock shows the amount of time you can expect to spend at your computer for each step. Naturally, you'll need much less time if you only read through the step rather than complete it at your computer.

You can also focus on particular points by scanning the short notes in the margins and locating the sections you are most interested in.

In addition, three symbols highlight particular sections of text:

The Action symbol highlights important steps that you will carry out.

The Tip symbol indicates a practical hint or special technique.

The Warning symbol alerts you to a potential problem and suggestions for avoiding it.

We have structured the Up & Running books so that the busy user spends little time studying documentation and is not burdened with unnecessary text. An Up & Running book cannot, of course, replace a lengthier book that contains advanced applications. However, you will get the information you need to put the program to practical use and to learn its basic functions in the shortest possible time.

We welcome your comments

SYBEX is very interested in your reactions to the Up & Running series. Your opinions and suggestions will help all of our readers, including yourself. Please send your comments to: SYBEX Editorial Department, 2021 Challenger Drive, Alameda, CA 94501.

Table of Contents

Step 1

Installing Windows 3.1

You used to install computer programs manually by copying the program disks. Today's programs are too large and can't be installed manually, however. For this reason, easy-to-use installation programs are provided. They will help you complete the installation process and copy only those files that are absolutely necessary. Installation programs are comfortable to use and make installation easier for beginners.

This book assumes you have a basic knowledge of computers. You should already have some experience with PCs and DOS as well. To make sure you read this book without any difficulty, and to make sure you understand the installation procedure, I would like to review and clarify the most important basic computer terms.

The computer stores data in files, and each file has a file name that uniquely defines it. A file name can be as long as eight characters, plus a period and a three-character file extension. File extensions are used to describe file types. For example, the extension in DEMO.DOC tells you that the file is a "document."

File

Files are organized in directories. A floppy disk or a hard disk can hold many directories. In order to access a file, you must know in which directory it is stored. Many programs produce new directories independently for managing their work data.

Directory

Computers store data on magnetic storage devices, such as floppy or hard disks. You access these devices by way of disk drives. On the drives are directories that contain files. Each drive has its own drive designation: the first floppy disk drive is called drive A, the second one (if available) is called drive B, the first hard disk is called drive C, and so on.

Drive

A path is a combination of a drive, directory, and file name. Through paths you define where information is found.

Path

These days, along with copying files, the installation procedure addresses your computer's *configuration*. Configuration refers to the individual requirements of the user, as well as the abilities of his or her particular computer and its peripherals.

No prior knowledge required

Windows 3.1 is quick and easy to install thanks to its interactive installation program. No previous knowledge of Windows is required because the installation program takes care of as much as possible automatically. Predefined settings can be corrected later at any time, so you can accept the Windows 3.1 default settings without further consideration. Windows 3.1's fully automatic installation requires hardly any user-supplied information.

System Requirements

In theory, Windows 3.1 can run on any PC that is equipped with at least an 80286 processor. In fact, there are minimum requirements for the amount of available memory and the amount of hard-disk storage capacity. The following conditions must be met in order to install Windows 3.1:

In Enhanced mode

In Standard mode

- MS-DOS or PC-DOS Version 3.1 or higher.

- A PC with an 80386 (or higher) is required to run Windows 3.1 in Enhanced mode. The PC must have at least 2 Mb of available RAM (640K of base memory and 1024K of extended memory).

- A PC with an 80286 (or higher) is required to run Windows 3.1 in Standard mode. The PC must have at least 1 Mb of RAM (640K of base memory and 256K of extended memory).

- A hard disk with at least 10 Mb of available disk space.

The conditions described here are checked during installation. If there isn't enough available space on the hard disk, for instance, you will see an error message to tell you as much.

Making Backup Copies

Before you install Windows 3.1, you should make backup copies. Start your computer as usual and enter the following command:

```
diskcopy a: b:
```

If your computer happens to have only a single floppy disk drive, or two floppy disk drives of different sizes, copy the Windows disks with the following command:

```
diskcopy a: a:
```

Copy all the Windows disks in this way, label the disks accordingly, and put the original disks away in a safe place. Work only with the copies.

Starting the Installation

To install Windows 3.1 on your computer, use the Setup program, which is found on the first Windows disk. You can choose between two methods of installation: Express Setup or Custom Setup. I recommend Express Setup if you are in a hurry or have little experience. If you are an experienced Windows user, install Windows 3.1 with the Custom Setup program. But what are the differences between the two?

With Express Setup, the installation program recognizes the hardware and software of the system automatically, and Windows is configured accordingly. You still have to answer some unavoidable questions, such as which printer is connected to your computer. Everything else is done automatically.

Express Setup installation

With Custom Setup, you can influence the installation procedure. You can decide, for example, which system files to copy—and thereby save a good deal of hard disk space. Or you can make alterations to the DOS-system AUTOEXEC.BAT and CONFIG.SYS files. Custom Setup installation is recommended only for experienced users.

Custom Setup installation

Starting the Setup Program

To begin installing Windows 3.1, start your computer and put the first Windows disk in the floppy drive. Then enter the following information:

```
a:
setup
```

If you are installing Windows using the second floppy drive, use B: as the drive designation instead of A:. Now the Setup program starts, and an opening screen with some introductory information appears. Press the Enter key to confirm that you want to install Windows 3.1.

You can get context-sensitive help—that is, advice relating to the current operation, whatever it is—by pressing F1. You can terminate the installation procedure at any time by pressing F3.

Express or Custom Setup?

Now you choose between the Express or Custom Setup program. Less experienced users should press Enter to select Express Setup; experienced users can control the installation by pressing C for Custom Setup. I will assume that you have chosen the Express Setup. Custom Setup is explained later in this step under the heading "Custom Setup Installation."

Directory name for Windows

Next you define the directory name for Windows 3.1, normally C:\WINDOWS. If you want to install Windows 3.1 on another drive or in a different directory, change the directory name accordingly.

An error message will appear after you enter the path if there isn't enough free space on the hard disk drive you specified. To remedy this, either select another hard disk drive or clear off enough space on the one you selected. Windows 3.1 requires between 8 and 10 Mb.

Replacing an Existing Copy of Windows 3.0

The Setup program will recognize if Windows 3.0 is already installed on your computer. It will suggest replacing the old Windows version with Windows 3.1. In this case, simply confirm the suggested directory name. When you replace, or upgrade, an existing Windows version, the following happens:

- All program groups and program items in the Program Manager, including those that were added over the course of time, remain absolutely unchanged.

- All selected Windows system settings remain intact, such as the graphics adapter, mouse type, keyboard type, keyboard layout, and network.

- All the active Windows-specific device drivers are brought up to date automatically; third-party device drivers will *not* be replaced—you must do so manually later on.

- All required corrections and additions to the DOS-system AUTOEXEC.BAT and CONFIG.SYS files are made.

Upgrading from version 3.0

If for any reason you want to install Windows 3.1 without replacing Windows 3.0, simply reject the suggested directory name and enter another one, such as C:\WIN31. Barring a compelling argument not to upgrade, you should definitely replace the existing version.

Copying Windows to the Hard Disk

The Setup program now ascertains the configuration of your computer, which can take several seconds. If you decided on Custom Setup, the information ascertained will be displayed in detail (see "Custom Setup Installation" below); otherwise the installation proceeds directly.

Configuration

Now the Setup program begins installing Windows by copying the necessary system files. You are asked to insert additional floppy disks during the installation, as for example:

Changing Disks

```
Please insert the disk labeled
Microsoft Windows 3.1 Disk #2
         into Drive A:
   * Press Enter when ready
```

As soon as the first floppy disk is copied, the graphical user interface of Windows 3.1 becomes active. In the second part, Windows 3.1 is made to fit your individual preferences. The Setup program next requests your name, so that the Windows disks can be uniquely marked as yours.

Installing with the mouse

You are prompted to insert more Windows disks. As before, press Enter after you've inserted the required disk. You can also install Windows with the mouse. To do so, find the button on the screen marked OK, move the mouse cursor over the OK button, and click the left mouse button instead of Enter after you've inserted the disk.

Selecting a Printer

Now you must tell Windows which printer is connected to your computer. The Setup program provides an alphabetical list of all printers supported by Windows 3.1, as shown in Figure 1.1. Select your printer with the mouse or keyboard, and confirm your choice by pressing the Enter key or by clicking Install.

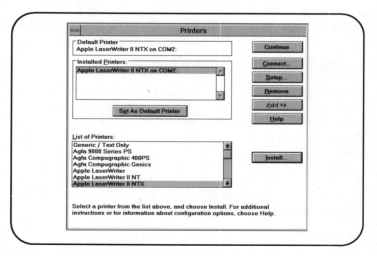

Figure 1.1: Selecting a printer

Next, the Setup program needs to know to which port your printer is connected. Most printers are connected to LPT1:, but some (chiefly laser printers) are connected to COM1:. If you are not certain to which port your printer is connected, consult your printer's manual.

Port

After installing the printer, the Setup program begins searching for applications on the hard disk. It organizes all Windows and DOS applications into program groups. The Setup program can store up to fifty applications in a program group. The first one is given the name "Applications," the second "Applications 2," and so forth.

Finding existing applications

The Setup program installs special PIF files for all non-Windows applications (DOS applications) it finds. PIF files are necessary for Windows to be able to run DOS applications without complications. DOS applications now have their own individual icons—a new feature of Windows 3.1.

At the end of the installation session, the Setup program offers you several Windows tutorials, including one for becoming familiar with the mouse. You can take advantage of this training now or at any time later on.

Windows tutorial

After you've installed Windows, you have the choice of starting the program (Reboot) or returning to the DOS interface (Return to MS-DOS). If you want to work with Windows 3.1 right away, select Reboot. Starting Windows is described in Step 2.

Starting Windows

Custom Setup Installation

By choosing Custom Setup instead of Express Setup, you can influence the installation in several ways. For example, you can change the configuration that is automatically provided, or make alterations to the DOS-system AUTOEXEC.BAT and CONFIG.SYS files. You can also tell the Setup program exactly which files to copy. This section describes what you need to consider when you opt for Custom rather than Express Setup.

Your first task with Custom Setup is to look at the displayed configuration, as shown in Figure 1.2. If any of the values need

Working on the configuration

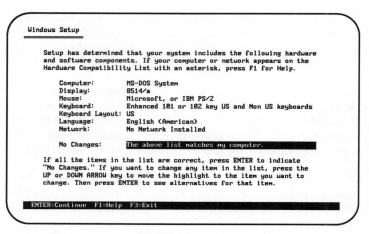

Windows Setup

Setup has determined that your system includes the following hardware
and software components. If your computer or network appears on the
Hardware Compatibility List with an asterisk, press F1 for Help.

Computer: MS-DOS System
Display: 8514/a
Mouse: Microsoft, or IBM PS/2
Keyboard: Enhanced 101 or 102 key US and Non US keyboards
Keyboard Layout: US
Language: English (American)
Network: No Network Installed

No Changes: The above list matches my computer.

If all the items in the list are correct, press ENTER to indicate
"No Changes." If you want to change any item in the list, press the
UP or DOWN ARROW key to move the highlight to the item you want to
change. Then press ENTER to see alternatives for that item.

ENTER=Continue   F1=Help   F3=Exit

Figure 1.2: The current configuration

changing, use the ↑ or ↓ keys to select the field. Next, press Enter
and correct the contents. As a rule, you will see a list with entries
from which you can select an appropriate one manually. When the
displayed configuration agrees with that of your computer, confirm
it by selecting

The above list matches my computer.

After the Setup program has copied the first disk, it asks what you
would like to control during installation. By clicking the mouse,
you can tell the Setup program which tasks to run automatically
and which ones you want to control. For instance, you might copy
only some system files in order to save space on your hard disk, or
you might install more than one printer.

Selecting specific files

You can determine in detail which file groups (Readme Files,
Accessories, Screen Savers, or Wallpapers) or which individual
components of these groups to copy. Activate or deactivate individual file groups by using the check boxes. By using the scroll bar
marked Files you can specify individual files. Use this feature only
if you are already experienced with Windows.

Next, the Setup program recommends a swap file. (The swap file is used by Windows to expand the amount of available memory. Data is "swapped" to a temporary file on the hard disk that would normally be stored in RAM.) You can either confirm this swap file or create one of your own. Besides determining on which drive to locate the swap file, you can determine how large it should be (in megabytes) and whether it should be permanent or temporary.

Swap file

After copying the system files, a window like the one in Figure 1.3 appears. Here, you determine how to make the necessary modifications to the two DOS system files. You can either allow the Setup program to make the changes, make the changes at this time, or make them later. As a rule, I recommend the first option. The Setup program will modify the two files as necessary to make Windows 3.1 operate efficiently. You can, of course, make changes to these files at any time in the future. Experienced users may prefer the second option, which allows you to edit the files directly on the screen.

Modifying AUTO-EXEC.BAT and CON-FIG.SYS

Finally, the Setup program searches for applications on the hard disk. Except when using Express Setup, you can decide which drives to search by choosing them with the mouse. After the Setup program has searched the selected drives, the names of the applications appear in a dialog box. You can confirm each application one by one. Only applications that you confirm will appear later in the Applications program group.

Searching for applications

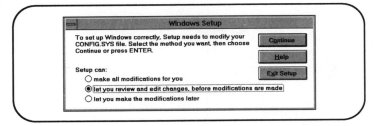

Figure 1.3: Modifying AUTOEXEC.BAT and CONFIG.SYS

Windows 3.1 has two operating modes, Standard mode and Enhanced mode. This step explains their differences, which operating
mode Windows 3.1 selects automatically, and how you can override
the automatic selection when necessary.

Windows 3.1 Operating Modes

If you have worked with Windows 3.0, you may wonder why we are
only discussing two operating modes. Starting with Windows 3.1,
Real mode has been abandoned. It caused too many problems in the
past. Because Real mode is no longer supported, the minimum
hardware requirement under Windows is an 80286 processor.

Standard Mode

Standard mode requires a PC with an 80286 processor (or higher)
and at least 1 Mb of RAM divided into 640K of base memory and
256K of extended memory.

Several Windows applications can run simultaneously in Standard
mode. DOS applications run exclusively as full-screen applications
and not concurrently with other applications.

Enhanced Mode

Enhanced mode is the most powerful operating mode in Windows 3.1.
It requires a PC with an 80386 processor (or higher) and at least 2
Mb of RAM divided into 640K of main memory and 1 Mb of
extended memory.

Because the 80386 processor supports virtual memory management, the Windows applications in Enhanced mode can access more
memory than is actually physically available. To expand the available working memory, a "swap file" is set up on the hard disk.

*Virtual
memory
manage-
ment*

*DOS
applica-
tions in a
window*

In Enhanced mode, you can load several DOS applications at the same time, and run them as windowed applications, with each application appearing in its own window on-screen. This is when you can really see the advantage of the graphical user interface. You no longer have to switch between text and graphics mode, and you can control several DOS applications on-screen simultaneously.

*Determin-
ing active
mode*

To find out in which mode Windows is currently working, select the About Program Manager option on the Help menu of the Program or File Manager. A window like the one in Figure 2.1 appears on-screen to tell you which mode is active and how much memory is available.

Starting Windows

Windows 3.1 can be started in either Standard or Enhanced mode. When you start the program, Windows determines which mode is best by checking what CPU is installed and how much memory is available. It chooses whichever mode is optimal, although you can choose the operating mode yourself if you wish, as will be explained shortly.

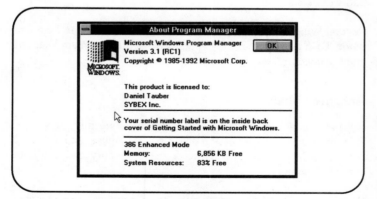

Figure 2.1: Determining the operating mode

Start Windows 3.1 by entering the following command at the DOS prompt:

WIN

Starting Windows 3.1 in a Specific Mode

Sometimes you'll want to start Windows in a specific mode. For instance, if your computer is equipped with an 80386 processor and 2 or 3 Mb of RAM, Enhanced mode is normally recommended (and would be chosen automatically). If you want to use Windows applications only—that is, if you won't be using DOS applications—Standard mode is recommended because you can achieve a faster operating speed.

You can't switch operating modes while Windows is running. Whichever operating mode you choose when you start Windows is active until you leave the program.

To let Windows choose the operating mode, just enter the WIN command without any additional information. However, if you want to select the operating mode yourself, enter one of the following options when you start Windows:

Options for setting the operating mode

/S   Starts Windows 3.1 in Standard mode. Select this mode if your computer is equipped with an 80386 processor (or higher) and 2 or 3 Mb of RAM, or if you plan to run Windows applications exclusively. Standard mode is also recommended if you are experiencing compatibility problems, for example, with your hardware.

/3   Starts Windows 3.1 in Enhanced mode. You can only start Windows 3.1 in Enhanced mode by using the /3 option if you don't have the normally required 2 Mb of RAM. An 80386 processor (or higher) is required in any case.

For example, if you wanted to start Windows in Standard mode, you would enter

WIN /S

If you try to start Windows 3.1 in an operating mode that is not available for your particular computer, an error message will appear on the screen.

If Windows 3.1 can be loaded in the operating mode you selected, the Program Manager will appear as usual on the screen. You can determine whether the operating mode you selected is indeed active by using the Help menu.

Starting Windows 3.1 with Other Applications

When you start Windows 3.1, you can have an application start at the same time. If, for example, you wanted to run Paintbrush directly after starting Windows 3.1, you would enter

```
win c:\windows\pbrush.exe
```

If you also wanted to load a document as well, you would enter the document name as another parameter:

```
win c:\windows\pbrush.exe paper.bmp
```

Naturally, along with the application, you can also specify the operating mode. To start Paintbrush and the PAPER.BMP document in Enhanced mode, you would enter

```
win c:\windows\pbrush.exe paper.bmp /3
```

Leaving Windows 3.1

If you want to leave Windows 3.1, use the mouse to select the Exit option on the File pull-down menu. If you are working with the keyboard, press Alt-F4, which has the same effect.

A dialog box appears on the screen asking you to verify that you actually want to leave Windows. The dialog box appears in order to prevent you from exiting by accident. Select OK to verify the exit. You will be returned to the DOS level.

Step 3

Working with Windows

Windows 3.1 gets its name from the windows it uses to display data. In this step you'll be introduced to the two types of windows, the application window and the document window. You'll also learn how to work with windows, how to position windows on the screen, and how to alter their size.

A window can only display an excerpt, or part, of a program or application. Using windows, you can determine which excerpt or part you would like to view. Let's look at the two types of windows, the applications window and the document window.

Types of Windows

In an *application window,* you look "into" an application. For instance, you could look into the Program Manager, the Write word-processing program, or the Paintbrush paint program. The name of the application you're viewing appears in the title bar of the window. If you have loaded a document into the application you're viewing, the name of the document will usually appear after the name of the application.

You can position an application window anywhere on the screen. You can also overlap application windows, either fully or partially. When you need a particular application window, you can always move it to the foreground. Only in Enhanced mode can you run DOS applications in their own windows.

The application window

The *document window* is the one that contains the current document, for example text or a picture. Each document window on-screen is assigned to a specific application.

The document window

You can recognize a document window because, unlike an application window, it doesn't have any pull-down menus of its own. Figure 3.1 shows the difference between document windows and application windows. A document window is always contained

Recognizing window types

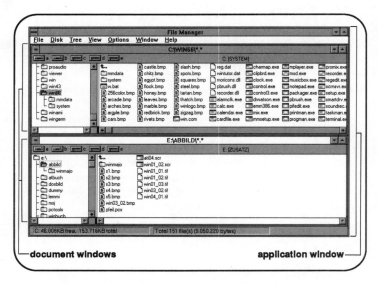

Figure 3.1: An application window and two document windows

within the frame of its corresponding application window, and it can't be moved out of that frame.

Some applications, such as Write and Paintbrush, only allow you to work on one document at a time. If you want to work on several documents at once with these applications, you must load the application several times over, once for each document you want to work on. Some applications, such as Word for Windows, let you open several windows at a time and work on several documents. The Program Manager also allows you to open several group windows (group windows are typical document windows).

Manipulating Windows

Changing window size and position

You can position most windows to any size nearly anywhere on the screen. With just a keystroke you can enlarge a window to full-screen size or restore it to its original size.

Application and document windows provide essentially the same capabilities, so you don't really need to differentiate between them when you work with windows. There are a few small differences to consider if you are using the keyboard, however. But before discussing the use of windows, lets look at the essential window elements.

The Window Elements

Figure 3.2 shows a typical application window. The individual elements of the window are identified with labels. Let's look at the elements of a window one by one.

The *Control menu box,* located in the upper-left corner of the window, accesses a special Control menu for functions such as closing and moving windows. If you are using the keyboard instead of the mouse, you will use the Control menu. With the mouse, you can move, close, or resize a window without the Control menu box. Use this box if you are using the keyboard.

Control menu box

On the *menu bar* of the application window you find the pull-down menus offered by the current application. The items that appear on

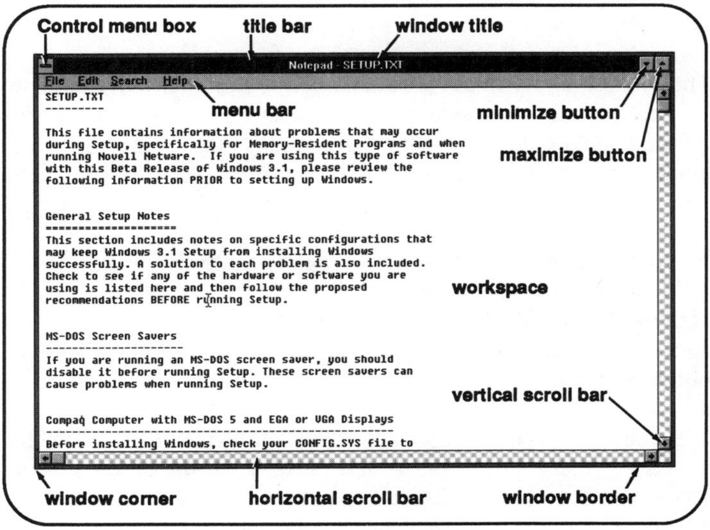

Menu bar

Figure 3.2: The elements of a window

the menu bar vary from application to application. However, most applications offer at least the File, Edit, and Help menu items. Additional menu items appear depending on the needs and purposes of the application.

Title bar

The *title bar* tells you, among other things, which window is the active one. The title bar of the active window appears in a highlighted color. The title bar also shows the name of the program or document.

Window title

The *window title* describes the contents of the window. Depending on the type of window, the window title can be the name of an application, a document, a directory, or a file. The name of the document currently being worked on appears after the name of the application. If the document has yet to be named, the word "Untitled" appears after the application name.

The workspace

The actual work with the application is carried out inside the *workspace*. This is where the contents of a document appear. If the application you're working with allows several document windows to be open at the same time, they can be moved only within the application's workspace.

Window border

The *window border* marks the outer edge of the window. It is used to change the window's size with the mouse. When you move the mouse pointer onto the window border, the mouse pointer changes into an arrow pointing up and down or left and right to let you know you can change window size.

Minimize button

You click the *minimize button* with the mouse to close the window and reduce it to an icon. The icon will be placed in the lower portion of the screen. In this way, programs can be "put on hold." The actual contents of the work remains undisturbed when you click the minimize button.

Maximize button

You click the *maximize button* in the Control menu box with the mouse to enlarge the window and make it fill the entire screen. When you click the maximize button of a document window, the window expands to the size of the existing application window. This is the maximum size to which it can expand.

In each corner of a window there are what appear to be slightly raised *window corners*. By placing the mouse pointer on one of these corners and dragging the mouse, you can change both the vertical and horizontal size of the window at once.

The *horizontal scroll bar* (sometimes called a *slider* or *slider box*) allows you to move the contents of a window display horizontally. The horizontal scroll bar usually appears only when all the contents of a document can't be displayed at once.

The *vertical scroll bar* allows you to move the contents of a window display vertically. Not every window has a vertical scroll bar.

Not every window has all of the elements described here. For example, not every window has scroll bars because Windows 3.1 doesn't display them if the entire contents of the document can be displayed in the document window. If the window is too small to show all the contents, then scroll bars appear.

Moving and Resizing Windows

Windows 3.1 can be operated comfortably not only with the mouse, but also with the keyboard. However, to use the keyboard you must learn a few key combinations. The following table shows the essential key combinations for operating windows.

Keys	Function
Alt-Spacebar	Opens the Control menu of the currently active application window.
Alt-Hyphen	Opens the Control menu of the currently active document window.
Alt-F4	Closes a window.

Table 3.1: Keys Used in Operating Windows

Keys	Function
Alt-Tab	Switches to the last application used or the next application running as an icon. You can cycle through currently active applications by repeatedly pressing Alt-Tab. Minimized applications are started as soon as they are selected.
Alt-Esc	Switches to the next application.
Ctrl-F6	Moves to the next group window.

Table 3.1: Keys Used in Operating Windows (continued)

To operate a window—that is, to change its size or position—you must call up its Control menu and select a menu item. You can't manipulate windows directly with the keyboard.

Moving Windows and Changing Their Size

To move or resize a window from the keyboard, proceed as follows:

The Control menu

1. If you are working in an application window, press Alt-Esc until the window you want to work with is active. If you are working in a document window, press Ctrl-F6.

2. Press Alt-Spacebar to activate the Control menu (with document windows, press Alt-Hyphen) and select a menu item with the↑ and ↓ keys or by pressing an underlined letter. You can

    - close the window,

    - reduce it to the size of an icon,

    - expand it to cover the full screen, or

    - change its position or dimensions.

3. A four-pointed arrow appears on the screen. Now change the size or position of the window.

4. Press Enter to end the procedure. The window will appear with the changes you made.

Reducing Windows to Icon Size

Suppose you need to close a window in order to create more room on the screen but you want the window's contents to remain accessible. You can do this by reducing the window to icon size (called *minimizing* the window). The icon will appear on-screen to remind you that the window is open and accessible although it is no longer visible.

*Minimizing
a window*

1. If you are working on an application window, press Alt-Esc until the window you want to minimize is active. If you are selecting a document window, press Ctrl-F6 instead.

2. Press Alt-Spacebar to activate the Control menu (with document windows, press Alt-Hyphen).

3. Select the Minimize item on the Control menu. The window will appear as an icon in the lower portion of the desktop (document windows appear in the lower portion of the corresponding application window).

Restoring Windows to Their Original Size

Because Windows keeps track of how big windows are, a window reduced to icon size can be restored to the size it was when you first minimized it. To restore a window to its original size,

1. Press Alt-Esc until you find the icon of the window you want to restore.

2. Press Alt-Spacebar to bring up the Control menu. With document windows, choose the appropriate document window with Ctrl-F6 and select the Control menu with Alt-Hyphen.

3. The icon's Control menu appears. To open the window again, select Restore or Maximize. Maximize restores a window not to its previous size, but to full-screen format.

Using the Mouse

Windows is a graphical user interface, and, as such, it was designed for use with a mouse. Many operations are done more quickly and easily with the mouse than with the keyboard. With the mouse, you can freely point to each window and icon that appears on the screen. The procedures described in the rest of this Step are all done with the mouse.

Moving Windows

To move a window, proceed as follows:

1. Position the mouse pointer anywhere on the title bar and click the left button. (If your mouse is configured for left-handers, click the right button.)

2. Hold the mouse button down.

3. A window outline appears. Move it where you want the window to be (document windows can only be moved within the corresponding application window).

4. Release the mouse button. Now the position of the window is set, and it is displayed in the new position.

Resizing Windows

To enlarge a window to full-screen size, click on the maximize button (the button with the upward-pointing arrow in the upper-right corner of the window.) To bring a maximized window back to its previously selected size, click on the maximize button again (it now has two arrows, one pointing up and the other down.) Clicking on this button restores the window to its original size.

To resize a window,

1. Position the mouse pointer on one of the four window corners or a side of the window. The mouse pointer changes to a four-pointed arrow.

2. Hold down the mouse button and drag the mouse to reshape the window.

3. Click the mouse.

Windows as Icons

If you want to close a window but keep the application behind it active, minimize it by clicking the minimize button in the upper-right corner of the window. This reduces the application to an icon. The icon will appear in the lower portion of the desktop.

To select an icon, position the mouse pointer on the icon and select it by double-clicking. The window will expand once more to its original size. You can make the icon's Control menu appear by clicking the mouse button only once while the mouse pointer is over the icon. From there you can select any of the menu items with the mouse.

Selecting icons

To move an icon, position the mouse pointer on the icon and hold the mouse button down. Next, drag the icon where you want it to be on the desktop. As soon as you let go of the mouse button, the icon will be displayed at its current position.

Moving icons

Step 4

Understanding Dialog Boxes

In Windows 3.1, you choose commands and functions with the keyboard or the mouse. The complicated command sequences on the keyboard that are a feature, for example, of DOS are no longer necessary. However, Windows 3.1 can't get by without some user-supplied information. For instance, you may need to specify a file name, choose between various options, or simply confirm an error message. In all of these cases, a dialog box appears on the screen in Windows 3.1. In this step you will learn how to use a dialog box with the keyboard and the mouse.

Working with Dialog Boxes

Dialog boxes usually appear in the middle of the screen. They are made of various components. For example, when you select the Open option on the File pull-down menu, the Open dialog box appears, as shown in Figure 4.1. Almost every Windows application has an Open dialog box. Dialog boxes also appear when Windows displays an error message or warning. As a rule, though, error-message dialog boxes only require you to acknowledge the message; further information usually isn't required.

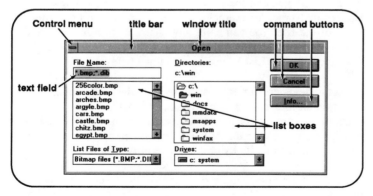

Figure 4.1: A typical dialog box

Like every application and document window, each dialog box has a title bar, window title, and Control menu. Most dialog boxes can be moved on the screen, but cannot be resized because of their fixed dimensions.

Moving dialog boxes

To move a dialog box with the mouse, simply place the mouse pointer on the title bar, click the mouse, and move the dialog box. If you are using the keyboard, activate the Control menu by pressing Alt-Spacebar and select Move. Next, move the dialog box with the cursor keys.

Command buttons

Dialog boxes always have various *command buttons*. Command buttons indicate which options are available to you. Two command buttons, OK and Cancel, almost always appear in dialog boxes.

- If you want to confirm the message in a dialog box, press the OK command button.

- To abort the task of the dialog box and reject any input up to that point, press Cancel.

A command button that is not available appears dimmed. You can't select a command button that is dimmed.

Text fields

In Figure 4.1 you can see various types of *text fields* or *text boxes*. Under File Name, for example, you see a text field for entering the name of the file. You can enter any character in most text boxes. Either enter the information with the keyboard or choose an item from the list box. (List boxes are explained below.)

Numeric fields

Numeric fields are for entering numeric values. A numeric value might be an integer, a decimal value, or a date, depending on the situation. In some cases, the numeric value can be established either by typing a value with the keyboard or by increasing or decreasing the value incrementally by pressing one of two buttons.

List boxes

Underneath the File Name and Directories text fields in Figure 4.1 you see examples of list boxes. In a list box, a list of existing items is displayed, usually in alphabetical order. You can choose an item from the list box instead of typing it in directly. If there are more items in the list than can be displayed at once, a scroll bar appears at the right side of the list box. Scroll through the list and find the item you want.

Besides multi-line list boxes, there are single-line list boxes. These are used when there is not enough room to display a multi-line list box in a dialog box. To the side of each single-line list box is a button with a downward pointing arrow. When you select this button, a list appears with entries to select from. The entry you choose will appear in the data field (unlike multi-line list boxes, where the entry you select is highlighted).

Single-line list boxes

You can see *option buttons*, another common feature of dialog boxes, in Figure 4.2. Only one option button can be selected at a time; the available options are therefore presented as "either-or." The currently selected entry is filled in.

Option buttons

Don't confuse option buttons with *check boxes*, which can also be seen in Figure 4.2. A check box determines whether an option is turned on or off. You can tell check boxes from option buttons because the option buttons are enclosed in a frame, like list boxes, to make it clear that they are to be viewed as a unit.

Check boxes

Here and there you will find scroll bars for entering numeric values, especially when a relative value like slow or fast, or 0 to 100 percent, is required. With this type of scroll bar, you click on one side or the other to establish the value you want.

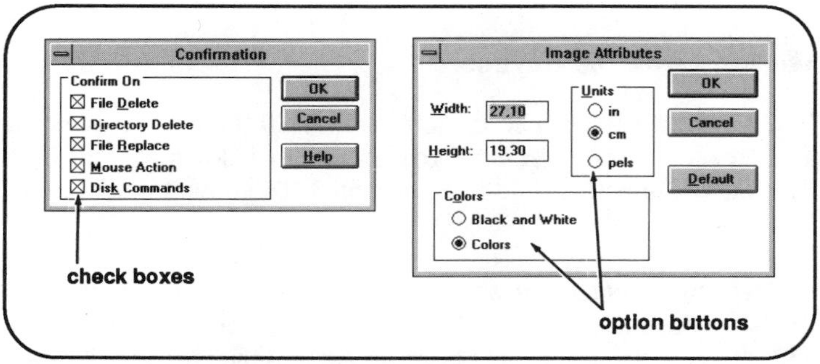

Scroll bars for relative input

Figure 4.2: Examples of check boxes and option buttons

Using Dialog Boxes

Using a dialog box is simple. When a dialog box first comes up, the cursor appears in the first field. From then on you can work on each field with the keyboard or the mouse.

Working with the Mouse

With the mouse, you can reach any field by pointing to it directly with the mouse pointer. Scroll bars work as they do with normal windows. Check boxes, option buttons, and command buttons can be selected directly with the mouse as well. Do so by clicking on the check box or option button with the mouse.

With check boxes and option buttons, you can just click on the text—you don't need to hit the button exactly. With command buttons, you have to click on the button itself.

Canceling a selection

If you position the mouse pointer and are holding down the mouse button but discover you've positioned the mouse on the wrong field, option button, or command button, just move the mouse pointer away from the field and release the mouse button.

Positioning the cursor in a text box

When you position the mouse pointer in a numeric field or text box, the field is selected automatically. The cursor is placed in the character position in the field that corresponds to the location of the mouse pointer.

Working with the Keyboard

Moving from field to field

You can move from field to field with the Tab key. As you press Tab, the cursor moves from left to right and then downward through the fields. The active field is hightlighted. To go backwards, press Shift-Tab.

Shortcut keys

Underlined letters often appear in the names of the individual fields—these underlined letters represent shortcut keys. Press the underlined letter in combination with Alt and the cursor will move directly to the field. For example, after choosing the Open item from the File pull-down menu, you could press Alt-D (*D* being the underlined letter in "Directories") to choose the Directories list box.

In text boxes and numeric fields, enter values with the keyboard. Use the ↑ and ↓ keys in check boxes and scroll bars. In list boxes and single-line list boxes, select the item you want with the ↑ and ↓ keys as well.

Entering informa- tion

Using the Command Buttons

Dialog boxes contain many command buttons, at the very least the OK command button and usually several others. Not all command buttons are available to you at all times. If, for instance, insufficient data is given to complete an entry, the OK button appears gray or dimmed. That means the button can't be used at the moment. When the required information is given and the entry is complete, the OK command button will appear in black letters.

Command buttons whose labels end with an ellipsis (...) or two angle brackets (>>) call up a second dialog box. The second dialog box appears because, in order to carry out the function, more information is required. Once the information in the second dialog box is confirmed, you can continue working in the current dialog box.

When additional input is required

In Figure 4.3 you will recognize many elements of a typical dialog box. All command buttons except Add >> can be selected.

In every dialog box there is a default command button that is activated when you press Enter. While the Esc key always stands for Cancel, Enter can be assigned to many different commands. It doesn't always activate the OK command.

Default keys

Usually, pressing Enter activates the default command button. The default command button is framed with a wider border than the other command buttons. Of course, only an available command button can function as the default.

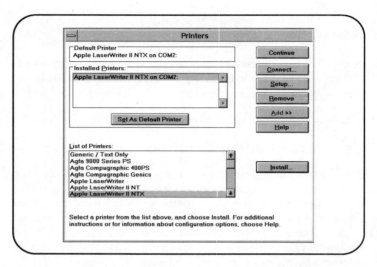

Figure 4.3: Unavailable command buttons are dimmed, or gray.

Knowing the default command button is only important when you are using the keyboard. With the mouse, you always select the specific key.

Pull-down menus are with you constantly as you work with Windows 3.1. Each window has a Control pull-down menu with numerous menu items, and each application provides a complete pull-down menu bar whose size is determined by the application's capabilities. Behind each menu item is a command or a function that Windows or the current Windows application carries out when the menu item is selected. This Step explores pull-down menus and how to use them.

The Control Menu

Application windows, document windows, application and group icons, as well as some dialog windows use the Control menu. You reach the Control menu by pressing Alt-Spacebar (in document windows, press Alt-Hyphen), or by clicking on the Control menu box in the upper-left corner of the window.

Let's look at the individual items on the Control menu more closely. Not every Control menu includes all of items described below, but all are included in case you encounter them in your work with Windows 3.1.

Restore	redisplays the window in its original size after a Maximize or Minimize operation.	*Control menu items*
Move	allows the window to be repositioned with the help of the keyboard.	
Size	allows the window to be resized with the help of the keyboard.	
Minimize	reduces the window to icon size.	
Maximize	enlarges the window to its maximum size.	
Close	closes the window.	

Switch To ...   displays the Task list.

Next   selects the next document window or icon in the application.

Selecting Menu Items

The techniques for working with menus are the same for the Control menu (see Figure 5.1) and for application pull-down menus. The only difference is that application pull-down menus offer several general headings, each of which, in turn, has any number of secondary menu items. The Control menu, on the other hand, does not have several general headings but is accessed directly through the Control menu box.

Selecting the Control menu

You can select the Control menu of an application window by clicking on the Control menu box, by pressing Alt-Spacebar, or by pressing Alt-Hyphen. An application's menus are accessed in the same way.

Working with the Mouse

Pulling down menus

To display the menu items behind a pull-down menu, position the mouse pointer on the pull-down menu's label and hold down the mouse button. To select a menu item, keep holding the mouse

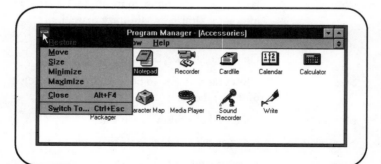

Figure 5.1: The Program Manager's Control menu

button down and pull the mouse pointer onto the item you want to select. When you release the mouse button, the highlighted menu item will be executed.

Selecting menu items

To pull down a menu and select the first item simultaneously, re-lease the mouse button immediately after you select the pull-down menu (as shown in Figure 5.2). You can now select another pull-down menu or one of the displayed menu items. To select a menu item, position the mouse pointer and press the mouse button. Now, the appropriate item is highlighted, and when you release the mouse button, the menu item will be selected and its actions carried out. If you decide not to select an item, don't release the mouse button. Instead, just move the mouse pointer.

Ending your work with menus

If you want to leave menu mode, click on any object with the mouse or on any occupied portion of the screen. Or, you can simply click on the active pull-down menu again. To close the Control menu, click again on the Control menu box.

Menu items that are not currently available appear dimmed. If you select such a menu item accidentally, the cursor will reappear on the first item in the menu.

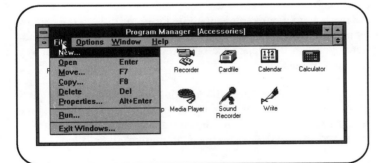

Figure 5.2: The application menus of the File Manager

Working with the Keyboard

Alt activates pull-down menus

Press the Alt key once to reach the menu bar (with some applications, you can use the F10 key as well). You can now use the pull-down menus with the help of the cursor keys, Enter, and Esc.

To pull down a menu, press Enter, ↑, or ↓. The menu items will appear. Now move the cursor to the item you want to select and press Enter.

Canceling a menu

To stop working with a menu, press either Esc or Alt. By pressing Alt, you leave the pull-down menu bar entirely. If you press Esc you go back up a level.

Shortcut Keys

If you are using the keyboard, you can take advantage of the shortcut keys on the pull-down menus. In each pull-down menu is an underlined shortcut key. Press the shortcut key letter in combination with the Alt key and the menu will be selected and displayed.

Besides pull-down menus, menu items often have shortcut keys as well. Menu-item shortcut keys are also activated in combination with the Alt key, which means that most menu items can be executed with only two key combinations. First you press the key combination for the pull-down menu and then you press the key for the menu item. For example, the File Open menu item is executed by pressing Alt-F and then O. When you press these key combinations, you can use uppercase or lowercase letters. The Shift key need not be pressed.

Once you activate a menu with the Alt key, you can reach the pull-down menu to the left or right of your present menu by pressing the ← or → key, respectively. When you reach the leftmost or rightmost menu and you press ← or →, the Control menu is selected.

Menu Conventions

In Windows 3.1, certain conventions are observed to ensure that menus are consistent with one another and that working with applications is made as easy as possible for the user. For example, File and Edit pull-down menus are found in nearly every application, and most applications present File and Edit as the first two menu items.

Besides command names, individual menu items often consist of additional information in the form of symbols. Symbols appearing after a menu command have the following meaning:

...	A dialog box appears on the screen if you select this menu item. The dialog box appears because Windows or the application requires additional information before it can execute the command.	*Menu symbols*
√	The option is currently active. If you select this menu item, the option is deactivated.	
▶	The menu item contains further submenu items; these will appear when you select the menu item.	
Keys	The menu item or command can also be selected by pressing the displayed key or key combination.	

Menu items that can't be selected appear gray or dimmed to distinguish them from other, accessible menu items. Selecting a dimmed menu item has no effect on the dialog box.

Unavail- able menu items

The Program Manager

Every operating system, every large application, and every graphical user interface has a control center similar to the cockpit of an airplane. In Windows 3.1, the *Program Manager* handles this function. The Program Manager is where you load Windows and DOS applications and manage the hard disk. It is where you control numerous Windows 3.1 capabilities.

Windows' cockpit

The Program Manager plays a similar role to the command interface of DOS: it controls the operating system and user interface and manages the system resources. The Program Manager is loaded automatically when you start Windows 3.1. You can't leave the Program Manager without leaving Windows 3.1.

The command interface

Working with Program Groups

Within the Program Manager are *program groups*. Each progam group contains a number of application programs, each of which is represented by a program icon. Thanks to program groups, applications can be readily organized and managed. You can set up a program group for each application, or group applications in broader categories. (For example, you could group all word processing programs in a Word Processing program group.) With this flexibility, everyone can set up his or her own control center.

Programs are grouped

Applications are represented in program groups by symbols called *program icons*. Program icons are usually descriptive. For instance, the Write text editor is represented by the nib of a pen, and the Paintbrush graphics program is represented by an artist's palette. To start an application, you simply select the icon.

Program icons

The Five Standard Groups

After you've installed Windows 3.1, five distinct program groups are usually set up—it can be four or more than five, however. These groups are described below.

Main group

The Main group contains the most important Windows 3.1 applications, including the File Manager or the Print Manager, but also Windows Setup, the Control Panel, the Clipboard, the PIF Editor, and the MS-DOS Prompt.

Accessories group

The Accessories group comprises various utility programs that come with Windows 3.1. These programs have nothing do with the operation of the graphical interface, but you can work with them as you would any other Windows application. Here you find, for instance, the Write word processor, the Paintbrush paint program, the terminal program Terminal, the Notepad, the Macro Recorder, the Cardfile, the Calendar, the Calculator, the Clock, the Character Map, the Media Player, and the Sound Recorder.

Games group

Windows 3.1 comes with two games. You can pass the time with Solitaire or try to keep one step ahead of the concealed mines in Minesweeper.

StartUp Group

The StartUp group is new. Applications you put in the StartUp group will be loaded automatically when you start Windows 3.1. Load your favorite programs and your favorite small utilities in this group.

Applications group

The Applications group comprises applications that are found beside the standard Windows 3.1 applications, such as Excel or Word for Windows. In Windows 3.1—unlike version 3.0—all DOS (non-Windows) applications are also kept in this group.

The Elements of the Program Manager

The Program Manager is composed of three elements—the group window, program icons, and group icons—as shown in Figure 6.1. Let's look at these elements one at a time.

The group window

A *group window* appears when you select—that is, you double-click on—a group icon. All the programs in the group you select are displayed in the group window. The size and position of a group window remain in memory when it is closed. Group windows, like

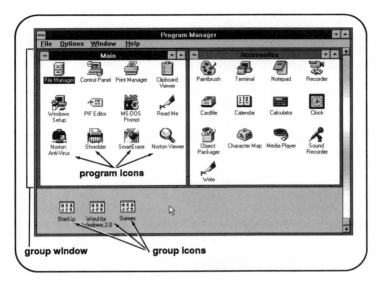

Figure 6.1: Elements of the Program Manager

document windows, have a Control menu and can be moved anywhere inside the application window of the Program Manager. You can change the size and position of a group window the same way you change the size and position of other types of windows.

Program icons

Every application in the group window is represented by a *program icon*. To start an application, select its icon. You can move or copy a program icon from one group window to another, but you can't "park" a program icon outside the group window in the Program Manager's application window, or outside the application window on the desktop.

Group icons

Every program group that doesn't appear in an open window can be accessed by way of its *group icon*. To open a program group, just double-click on its group icon. You don't need to open a group window to have access to a group's Control menu. Just press Alt-Hyphen or click on the group icon once with the mouse to make the group's Control menu appear.

*Opening a
program
group*

To open a group window, select the group icon with the mouse and double-click on it. The group window will appear. To do this from the keyboard, press Ctrl-Tab until you've selected the right group icon, and then press Enter. Alternatively, you can select the group window you want to work with from the Window pull-down menu. If the group window is not yet opened, it is opened automatically.

*Closing a
program
group*

To close a group window, double-click on the Control menu box, or select Close or Minimize from the Control menu. Alternatively, you can click on the window's close box. With the keyboard, you can close a group window via the Control menu or by pressing Ctrl-F4.

Unlike application windows, group windows are never completely closed or removed. They are simply "minimized" and appear at the bottom of the Program Manager window.

Creating or Expanding a Program Group

When you install Windows 3.1, several program groups like Main, Accessories, and StartUp are already set up. But you can also set up new program icons and even new program groups.

*Creating
a new
program
group*

To create a new program group,

1. Select New from the File pull-down menu.

2. A dialog box appears on the screen, in which you can choose whether to create a new program item or a new program group. A program item is an icon that represents an application, accessory, or document that will be shown in a group window. To add a new program group, select Program Group.

*Use short
names*

3. Define a name for the new group. Choose a short and practical name, so as not to take up needless space on the screen.

4. If you want to, specify a file name for the program's group file. The name of the group file is limited to eight characters, so don't specify a file extension. The Program

Manager creates a file with the extension .GRP in order to administer the group.

If you want to add a new application to a program group,

New program item

1. Select the group to which you want to add the application.

2. Select New from the File menu.

3. Specify that you want to create a new program icon (standard installation). Note that you can have no more than fifty program icons in each group.

4. A "Program Item Properties" window like the one in Figure 6.2 appears. First enter a description of the application; it should be as meaningful but brief as possible. If you don't enter a description, the program icon will be labeled with the application's name.

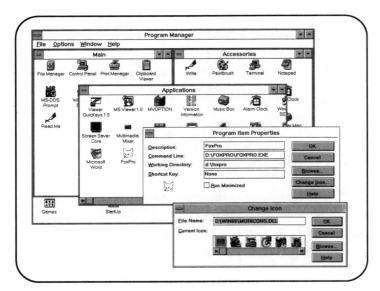

Figure 6.2: Defining a new program icon

Command Line

5. On the second line, enter the command line that is required to start the application. Include the complete path as well as any required parameters or options.

Searching for program files

- If you don't know the file name of the application, press the Browse command button. Windows will look for every application, in DOS as well as Windows. If Windows finds the desired application, it will select it and its name will appear in the Command Line of the dialog box.

- If the application you want to add to the program group isn't in the current directory or in a subdirectory specified with the DOS PATH command, you must specify the complete path in the Command Line field. For example, you would enter

  `c:\excel\execel.exe.`

Working Directory

6. In the Working Directory, define which directory you will be working in when the program icon is selected. The Working Directory field is new in Windows 3.1.

Shortcut Key

7. In the Shortcut Key field, you can specify a key combination to activate and also start the application. You can use the Ctrl-Alt, Ctrl-Shift-Alt, or Ctrl-Shift key combinations. As soon as you press the keys, they appear in the Shortcut Key field. For instance, you could use Ctrl-Alt-W to start Word for Windows when it isn't active, and to switch to it when it has already been started.

Run Minimized

8. Either check of leave blank the Run Minimized option. When this option is checked, the application is immediately minimized when you load it.

Change Icon...

9. With the help of the Change Icon feature, you can select a different icon for your application. Some Windows applications offer several icons from which to choose.

Changing a Program Icon's Properties

You can control an application's properties with the Properties option on the File menu. That is, you can change the options or parameters on the command line or select a different program icon. To change parameters, proceed as though you were creating a new program icon, and change the parameters in the "Program Item Properties" window.

Copying or Moving Program Icons

To copy or move a program icon, open both the group window from which you want to copy or move the icon (the source window) and the group window to which you want to move or copy it (the target window). Next, if you are using the mouse,

1. Point to the program icon you want to move or copy and hold down the mouse button.

With the mouse

2. To move the icon, drag it to the new group window and release the mouse button. To copy the icon, press the Ctrl key while you drag the program icon to the new program group.

With the keyboard

To move or copy a program icon with the keyboard,

1. Select the appropriate program icon.

2. Select the Copy menu item. (Alternatively, you can just press F8.)

3. A dialog box appears. Type in the name of the target program group.

Take care not to exceed the fifty-program limit when you move and copy program icons from one group to another. If you attempt to add more than fifty, you will receive an error message.

Maximum programs

Deleting a Program Icon

If you want to delete a program icon or program group, select the icon and press the Del key. Alternatively, you can select Delete from the File menu. After an obligatory confirmation for safety's sake, the program icon or group will be deleted.

Starting Applications in a Group Window

To start an application in a group window, select the group window or group icon that contains the application you want to start. If you have not done so already, you must select the group icon to open the group window. Next, select the program icon with the mouse or cursor keys, and double-click on the icon or press Enter. This starts the program.

Reducing the Program Manager to Icon Size

You can reduce the Program Manager's application window to icon size when you start an application. This is helpful for saving space on the screen. To reduce the Program Manager automatically when you start up an application, activate the Minimize on Use command on the Options menu of the Program Manager. The Program Manager icon will appear on the bottom line of the desktop, where it is visible and ready to be accessed after you load your applications.

You can assign several program icons to the same application in the Program Manager. For example, it would make sense to have three or four different program icons for starting Excel. One icon could start a worksheet, one a balance sheet, one the newest sales figures, and one the current inventory.

Returning to the Program Manager

If you want to return to the Program Manager from the application you're currently working with, there are several ways to do so:

- Close the application by selecting Exit from the File menu.

- Click in the Program Manager window or, if it's minimized, double-click on the Program Manager icon. With the keyboard, switch to the Program Manager by repeatedly pressing Alt-Esc.

- Activate the Task Manager.

Quitting the Program Manager

When you quit your work with the Program Manager, you also quit
Windows 3.1. The Program Manager is the highest command level
of Windows 3.1. That is why you can't leave the Program Manager
without leaving Windows 3.1.

Before you can leave the Program Manager, you must close all
currently running applications. The Program Manager closes
all open applications—except for DOS applications—automatically.
You can save any documents that have been changed. An appropriate confirmation dialog box appears on the screen, and finally you
will see the dialog box shown in Figure 6.3.

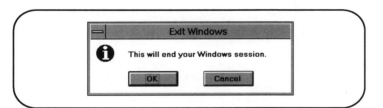

Figure 6.3: Confirming that you want to leave Windows

The File Manager

If you've worked with Windows 3.0, you will hardly recognize the new File Manager. The developers of Windows completely redesigned it. The File Manager is much easier to use and has several new capabilities. And, more importantly, the File Manager is much faster than before.

The File Manager's most important task is to manage and organize the disk drives, and thus to manage and organize directories and files as well. With the File Manager, you can not only look at the directory structure of a disk drive, you can also manage files comfortably. Of course, you can also start applications with the File Manager, and do much more besides. In this step I will describe how the File Manager functions, its essential elements, and its most important capabilities.

*File
Manager
tasks*

Starting the File Manager

Provided you have not rearranged the Main group, the File Manager's program icon will appear in the first position. It appears there because the File Manager plays a big role in managing hard disks—a role comparable to the many user interfaces available for that purpose under DOS.

To start the File Manager, select the File Manager icon in the Main group of the Program Manager. Do this by a double-clicking with the mouse. The File Manager starts up.

If you haven't worked with the File Manager before, a window appears to show you the directory structure of the current default drive and the contents of the default directory. If this isn't the first time you've started the File Manager, the window shows the same information it displayed when you last left the File Manager.

You can use the File Manager instead of the Program Manager as the user interface for Windows 3.1 by making a special entry to your SYSTEM.INI system file. Replace the file name (PROGRAM.EXE)

*The File
Manager
as user
interface*

that follows the SHELL command with WINFILE.EXE. The line will look like this:

```
SHELL=WINFILE.EXE
```

Windows will start not with the Program Manager, but with the File Manager. Of course, you can start the Program Manager from within the File Manager (and vice versa with the default installation).

Starting Windows 3.1 with the File Manager

If you already know when you start Windows that you want to work with the File Manager, you can start directly with the File Manager by entering this command line:

```
WIN WINFILE.EXE
```

The Organization of the File Manager

The structure of the File Manager is similar to that of the Program Manager. The File Manager itself is represented in an application window with a menu bar. Any number of document windows can be displayed within the File Manager's application window. As with the Program Manager, you can't move these windows outside the borders of the File Manager's window.

On the left side of the window you see the directory structure (or tree) of the drive being worked on; on the right side the contents of the directory are displayed. In Windows 3.0, you could only work with one disk drive, and only one directory tree was displayed.

The window

In each window you can work on a different drive. You can open more than one window for the same drive, however. The File Manager assumes that you want to see the directory tree *and* the directory contents, but you can close off one or the other. You can also adjust the size of the two parts of the window. To do this, you move the border between the directory tree and the directory contents like a movable partition.

The directory tree

Windows uses graphic elements to represent the directory structure of the currently displayed drive in the directory tree. The directory each other—is very clear. You are probably familiar with directory trees from having worked with DOS utilities or the DOS shell.

The right side of the drive window shows you the contents of the currently selected directory. Here, all file names and subdirectories are displayed. They are sorted by criteria that you can specify. If you minimize a drive window to icon size, the name of the appropriate directory will be displayed. This way, you can have quite a number of directories open without taking up a lot of space on the desktop.

*The
directory
contents*

The Elements of the File Manager

The most important elements of the File Manager are displayed in Figure 7.1. Below is a brief explanation of the various components of the File Manager.

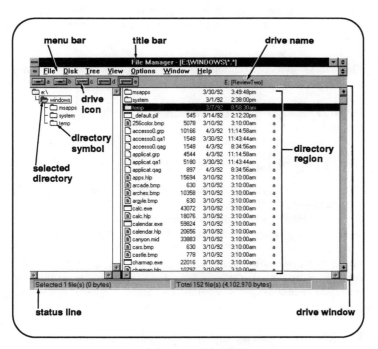

Figure 7.1: The structure of the File Manager

Title bar

The title bar includes the Control menu box and the pull-down menus as well. The menus offer numerous ways to affect how information is displayed. They also give you many options for working with drives, directories, and files.

Menu bar

The File Manager menu bar displays the directory structure on the left and the contents of the directory on the right.

Drive icon

Each logical drive designation, including RAM disks, CD-ROM drives, and network drives, is represented by a drive icon.

Drive name

The drive name, or volume label, as well as the drive's designation letter, is displayed to the right of the drive icons.

The selected directory appears highlighted in the directory tree.

Directory symbol

For every directory and subdirectory there is a symbol. The directory that is currently displayed in the window on the right is represented by an open folder.

Status line

The status line shows the total memory consumption and the available disk space of the current drive.

Directory region

In the Directory region, the file names and subdirectories of the currently selected directory appear.

Working with the Directory Tree

When you start the File Manager, at least one drive window is opened automatically. You can open as many drive windows as you want, each with its own directory tree. In this way, all drives and directories are easily accessible.

Selecting a drive

To select a drive with the mouse, position the mouse cursor on the drive icon and click the mouse button. The contents of the current drive window will be overwritten. By double-clicking on the drive window, you can make a new drive window appear.

To select a drive with the keyboard, press the Tab key until the highlighted drive icon is bordered by a small frame. Next, use the cursor keys to select the drive. Confirm by pressing Enter.

You can press the Ctrl key in combination with a drive letter to select a drive. The contents of the current drive window will be overwritten by that of the new one.

Changing the Default Directory

The name of the currently selected directory is shown in the title bar of the drive window. The current directory itself is highlighted in the directory tree. A new drive window is opened when you select the current directory.

You can select any directory or subdirectory with the mouse. If there isn't enough room to show them all in the directory region of the drive window, use the scroll bar to display the appropriate part of the directory tree. See Table 7.1 for a list of keys to use to move around in the directory tree.

Key	*Function*
Home	moves the cursor to the root directory.
End	moves the cursor to the last directory.
↓	moves the cursor to the next directory. (Ctrl-↓ selects the next directory of the same hierarchical level.)
↑	moves the cursor to the previous directory. (Ctrl-↑ selects the previous directory of the same hierarchical level.)
→	moves the cursor to the first subdirectory.
←	moves the cursor up one directory level.
PgUp	moves the cursor one page upward.
PgDn	moves the cursor one page downward.
Enter	opens a new window with the current directory.
Tab	moves between the directory tree and drive icons.

Table 7.1: Keys for Moving Around the Directory Tree

Key	Function
n	Selects the next directory that begins with the letter *n*, where *n* represents a letter of the alphabet.

Table 7.1: Keys for Moving Around the Directory Tree (continued)

Accessing Directory Tree Branches

Only sub-directories of the root directory

To prevent confusion, only the directories of the root directory are displayed by default in the directory tree. If you want to see whether a directory contains subdirectories of its own, double-click on the directory's folder or choose the Indicate Expandable Branches option on the Tree pull-down menu. A plus sign will appear on directory folders that contain subdirectories of their own.

If you want to view a subdirectory, click on the plus sign. Or, with the keyboard, choose the directory and then press the plus (+) key.

A minus sign appears on the directory folder icon when all of a directory's subdirectories are displayed. By clicking on the folder icon or pressing the minus (−) key, you can hide the subdirectories once more.

Sometimes the Indicate Expandable Branches option is not active. In this case, you can't tell whether a directory has any subdirectories. However, you can look in the contents portion of the drive window to the right, where the subdirectories will be displayed.

Working with Drive Windows

Directory name

The directory's contents are displayed in the right side of the drive window. If a directory has more subdirectories than can be displayed, you can select them and open additional windows. The title bar of the directory window shows the name of the directory being worked on. The size and position of the directory window varies like any other document window.

To the left of the file and directory names is an icon that defines the directory entry's type. There are different icons for directories, program and document files, as well as other less clearly definable files.

Table 7.2 lists the keys you can use to navigate through the directory contents with the keyboard.

Key	*Function*
Cursor keys	move the cursor.
PgUp	moves one page upward.
PgDn	moves one page downward.
Enter	opens a subdirectory or runs a program.
Home	moves to the first entry in the directory.
End	moves to the last entry in the directory.
Ctrl-/	selects all entries in the directory.
Ctrl-\	unselects all entries in the directory.
Shift-F8	makes a box around the current selection blink. You can move the box to another file or directory name to select more than one entry. Select each additional entry by pressing the spacebar. Press Shift-F8 to turn off the blinking box.
n	selects the next entry that begins with the letter *n*, where *n* is a letter of the alphabet.

Moving around the drive window

Table 7.2: Key functions in the Drive Window

Several drive windows can be open at one time, but only one can be current, or active. You can change the current window with the mouse by positioning the mouse pointer anywhere on the window and clicking the mouse button. With the keyboard, change the current window by pressing Ctrl-F6 or by selecting Next on the Window pull-down menu.

Changing the current drive window

Pressing Ctrl-F6 is the quickest way to change the current window, but if many windows are open, the Window menu is better.

Changing How File and Directory Names Are Displayed

File and directory names are normally displayed in alphabetical order. From the View menu, you can change the sort order of the entries to fit your needs. The entries can be sorted by name, type, file size, or by the date the file was last modified.

Determin-
ing what is
shown

You can also determine *what* information is displayed on the screen and whether or not to display all files. You can specify which files to display with the By File Type option. Beyond that, you can specify various attributes, so that, for example, subdirectories or program files are excluded from the display.

Splitting
windows

You can change the spatial relationship between directory and file lists by choosing the Split option on the View pull-down menu. A black vertical bar appears on the screen. By moving it with the mouse or cursor keys, you can determine how much room is available for the directory tree. You can usually change the way the window is split, because the File Manager automatically gives the directory tree more room than it needs. When you have adjusted the size of the two window portions to your liking, click the mouse button or press Enter to accept the new setting. If you later open another window, it will take on the proportions you set.

You can also split the window by pointing the mouse at the small black vertical bar at the bottom of the window, holding down the left mouse button, and dragging the window in the direction required.

If you move the vertical dividing bar too far to the left, you might make the directory tree vanish entirely. If that is what you want to happen, use the View menu instead of the dividing bar. It has options for choosing whether to show just the contents, or just the directory tree, or both.

Selecting Files

Files
must be
highlighted

Before you can work on one or more files—to copy, delete, or move them, for instance—you must mark them. Normally, files that are marked are highlighted. With the mouse or the keyboard you can mark whatever entries you like.

To mark several files, you have to use the keyboard as well as the mouse. If you simply click on a file, all previously marked files will no longer be marked. To mark several files, hold down the Ctrl key and click the mouse on whatever files you want. They will remain highlighted, as shown in Figure 7.2.

Marking several files

To mark a list of files, choose the first entry in the list. Next, hold down the Shift key and click on the last entry in the list. Now both entries and every one in between are selected. You can also select a list by moving from the last to the first entry.

Marking a list of files

With the keyboard alone, marking a list is a little more involved. First, press Shift-F8 to put the highlight bar into blinking mode. Next, select or unselect individual files by pressing the Spacebar. You can turn off this selection mode by pressing Shift-F8 once more.

After you have marked all the files, you can pull down the File menu and perform one of the commands on all the selected files.

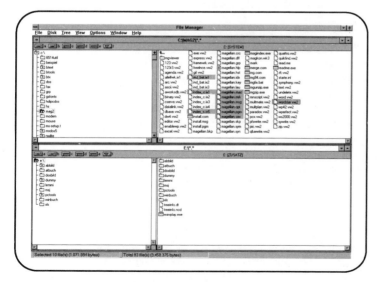

Figure 7.2: Selecting several files at once

Copying, Moving, and Deleting Files

Using a command from the File pull-down menu is not the only way to copy or move files. Using the mouse, it can be done much more simply and naturally:

Copying or moving files with the mouse

1. Point to the file that you want to copy or move.

2. Press the mouse button as usual and hold it down.

3. Depending on which action you want to take, hold down the Ctrl or Alt key:

   • To copy the selected files, hold down the Ctrl key.

   • To move the files, hold down the Alt key.

4. Drag the marked files to their destination. This can be a drive icon, a directory name, or even a program group of the Program Manager. If you are moving the file, the mouse cursor will change into a symbol representing a sheet of paper. If you are copying the file, the sheet of paper will display a plus sign.

5. Release the mouse button.

6. A dialog box appears on the screen. Confirm whether you intend to move or copy the file or files. Only after you confirm this action will it be carried out.

When you are moving or copying a file to another drive, you don't have to hold down either the Ctrl or Alt key.

Deleting files

To delete files, mark the files that you want to delete and press the Del key. A dialog box appears asking you to verify the command. As soon as you do so, the files will be deleted.

Drag and Drop

Some new catch-phrases are going around with Windows 3.1. One is "drag and drop." This phrase describes a welcome new feature whereby you handle data documents (files) separately from appli-cations. First you click on the desired document with the mouse, and then you drag it onto the already opened application (into the corresponding application window). Let's try it out:

1. Start the Write text editor.

2. Start the File Manager.

3. Organize the desktop so that Write is accessible.

4. Choose a file with the extension .WRI.

5. Click on this file with the mouse and "drag" the document into the Write text editor.

6. "Drop" the document by releasing the mouse button.

You can follow the same procedure with most other Windows applications, including Paintbrush and Notepad.

Leaving the File Manager

To leave the File Manager, select Exit from the File pull-down menu. A query will appear asking whether you want to save the current settings.

Step 8

Starting Applications

Unlike DOS, you can run several applications simultaneously with Windows 3.1. For example, while your spreadsheet program calculates and prints a difficult worksheet, you can simultaneously receive data with the Terminal program and write a letter with your word processor. However, in order for these procedures to be carried out at the same time you need a very fast computer.

Multitasking

When several applications are run simultaneously, the computer's resources—its memory, CPU time, etc.—are divided among the active applications. Running several applications simultaneously in Standard mode is only possible with Windows applications; DOS applications can be simultaneously loaded, but will not run in parallel. In Enhanced mode, you can run several non-Windows applications simultaneously, even in windows.

Multitasking with DOS applica- tions

Starting Applications

You start applications in various ways. The procedures are outlined below. Which one you follow to start a Windows or DOS application doesn't really matter. The procedures are different, but not the results.

Choose the program icon of the application you want to start (Paintbrush or Write, for example) from within the Program Manager's group window. Select the icon either with the keyboard and by pressing Enter, or by double-clicking on the icon with the mouse.

With the Program Manager

From within the File Manager, select a program file with the extension .EXE, .COM, or .BAT. Alternatively, you can select a PIF file (see Step 11 for more information on PIF files). Either mark the file with the cursor keys and press Enter, or double-click on the program file with the mouse.

With the File Manager

With the
File menu

Choose Run from the File menu of the File or Program Manager. Next, enter the command line to call up the program as you would from the DOS prompt.

With drag
and drop

You can also use the new drag and drop technique (which was introduced in Step 7).

Starting Applications with Run

If you are using the Program Manager, you can activate the Run command to start a program that is not assigned to an available program group. As a rule, you only use this command to start programs you seldom use.

After you select the Run command from the File menu, a dialog box appears on the screen as shown in Figure 8.1. Here, you are asked to enter a command line. The command line you enter corresponds to the DOS prompt or command line, and can therefore also contain a drive designation and path, as well as command line options and parameters. You can specify a document along with the application, such as a text file to be edited.

The
Browse
function

Notice the Browse function in the dialog box. This new function allows you to search your system for the application. You no longer have to know the drive and path of the application in advance, as you did in Windows 3.0.

Run Mini-
mized box

You can start more than one instance of the same application by activating the Run Minimized box. In this case, Windows doesn't

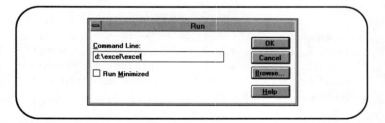

Figure 8.1: The Run dialog box

execute the command immediately, but puts an icon in the lower portion of the screen. You can select the icon at any time and as often as you want to start the application. When you leave Windows, the icon is erased and will no longer be on the desktop when you start Windows again.

Switching between Active Applications

Whether you have started several applications or have opened several windows, only one window can be *active*. You can tell which is the active window by its highlighted title bar. When several windows overlap, the active window is always the one in the foreground.

To switch to a new window, use the Alt-Esc key combination or the Switch To menu option on most Control menus to switch between opened windows and program icons until you've activated the window you want to work with. Alternatively, you can just select the window with the mouse. Position the mouse pointer in the appropriate window and click on the mouse button.

Switching applications

Pressing Alt-Esc switches immediately to the next application, but if you press Alt-Tab only the window title or icon is highlighted, as shown in Figure 8.2. At that point you can switch to the currently selected application simply by releasing the Alt key. This procedure is much quicker than Alt-Esc.

Using Alt-Tab is even faster if you have activated the Fast Alt+Tab Switching function in the Desktop area of the Control Panel. With that done, the name and the icon for the next application appears in the middle of the screen.

You can also activate a window with the Task Manager. In Step 9 you will find more information about this.

Task Manager

Starting the DOS Command Prompt

If you want to start the DOS command prompt, select the MS-DOS Prompt in the main group of the Program Manager. This way, you

Activating the DOS prompt

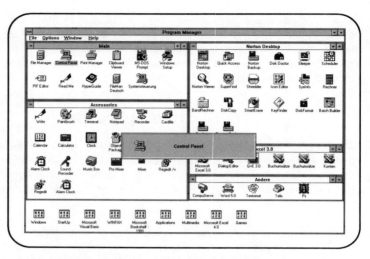

Figure 8.2: Switching applications with Alt-Tab

can reach the DOS command prompt without having to leave Windows. To do so, proceed as follows:

1. Start the Program Manager (if you haven't done so already).

2. Select the Main group.

3. Click on the MS-DOS Prompt icon with the mouse, or select it from the keyboard.

4. Work as you normally would with the DOS command interface. All DOS capabilities are at your disposal.

5. Return to Windows 3.1 by entering the EXIT command at the DOS prompt.

Switching back to Windows

From the DOS command interface, you can switch back to Windows without leaving DOS. Use the Alt-Esc or Alt-Tab key combinations. Your current work in DOS will be halted but not exited. In the lower portion of the desktop you will see a DOS icon with the description MS-DOS Prompt. If you want to return to DOS, just select the icon. Your halted DOS operations will then resume.

With this technique, you can set up several instances of the DOS command line and switch between them. Each DOS application is displayed as a full-screen application first. In Enhanced mode, however, you can run DOS applications in windows.

When you switch out of the DOS command interface, the application does *not* continue processing in the background; it is halted. Processing several DOS applications simultaneously is only possible in Enhanced mode.

Application "freezing"

To run a DOS application in a window, press Alt-Enter when the application is active. With this key combination you can switch between full-screen and windowed presentation.

Window application

Some commands—especially programs that influence the logical structure of the hard disk, such as Speed Disk, for instance, or the DOS command CHKDSK—should not be issued from the DOS command line.

To avoid complications, only call up such programs after you have left Windows. If you don't, the management of the hard disk structure could be scrambled under Windows. This applies also to all programs that restore lost files or optimize the hard disk structure—don't use these program until you've left Windows.

Step 9

The Task Manager

One strength of Windows is its ability to work with various applications at the same time. For example, while working with a database and a spreadsheet, you can download information with the Terminal program. Of course, you can also start more than one instance of a single application to work, for example, on several documents simultaneously. Individual applications that are worked on in parallel are called *tasks*. Processing several programs simultaneously is called *multitasking*.

Multitasking

Multitasking requires a powerful administrative expenditure, because the resources of the computer—its memory, drives, video, mouse, CPU time, etc.—must be divided evenly among the various tasks. It is the job of the Task Manager to do this. With the Task Manager, you can switch between various tasks, end a task, and also control how information is displayed on the screen.

Calling Up the Task Manager

There are three ways to call up the Task Manager:

- Double-click on a free position on the desktop—that is, outside of any windows.

- Select the Switch To option on the Control menu of any application.

- Press the Ctrl-Esc key combination.

The Task Manager's window doesn't always appear in the same position on the screen. If you activate it by double-clicking on the desktop, it will appear where you double-clicked. If you activate it with Ctrl-Esc, it will appear in the middle of the screen. If you use the Switch To option on the Control menu, it will appear below the menu.

To exit the Task Manager, close the window by pressing Alt-F4 or by clicking the Cancel command button. You can also exit the Task Manager by pressing Esc.

*Exiting
the Task
Manager*

The Structure of the Task Manager

The Task Manager is an application window and you can move it anywhere on the screen. You cannot change the window's size, however. The Task Manager essentially consists of the elements shown in Figure 9.1. Let's look at them one at a time.

Control menu box

The Control menu box of the Task Manager offers the Move and Close commands.

List of active tasks

The list of active tasks contains descriptions of the applications that have been started. If a document is being worked on by an application, the name of that document appears too. Windows provides a scroll bar if there isn't room to display all of the active applications.

Command buttons

Command buttons represent the various actions that can be carried out with the Task Manager. We will look at these buttons later in this Step.

Selecting the Active Window

The active window is the one that appears in the foreground. It can be accessed directly from the keyboard. As you have seen, you select the active window by clicking on the window or icon with the

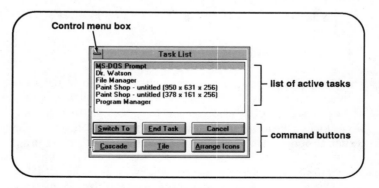

Figure 9.1: The structure of the Task Manager

mouse, by pressing Alt-Esc, or by pressing Alt-Tab. You can also use the Task Manager to select the active window. The Task Manager presents a user-friendly alternative for selecting a task, especially when many applications are running at once.

Selecting an application

To select an application, start the Task Manager by double-clicking or by pressing Ctrl-Esc. Next, choose the name of the application whose window you want to activate. You can move the selection bar through the list with the help of the cursor keys. To select a task, simply press Enter. If you are working with the mouse, double-click on the application. You can also click the Switch To command button.

Next, the corresponding window appears on the screen. If you selected an application that was minimized to icon size, the application's window will automatically be opened.

Choosing icons

Ending a Task

With the Task Manager you can end a task without having to disturb the Control menu of the given application. Ending a task with the Task Manager is especially useful if the application is "frozen" and can't react to the Exit command.

Terminating an application

To end a task, activate the Task Manager and select the appropriate task. Next, choose the End Task command button. To do this with the mouse, simply click on the corresponding button. With the keyboard, press Tab until the End Task button is highlighted, and press Enter.

If the application you want to close was modifying a document, you will be asked whether the document should be saved.

The Task Manager's Command Buttons

The first three command buttons of the Task Manager—Switch To, End Task, and Cancel—have already been described above in this

Step. Let's look at the other command buttons.

Cascade

Pressing the Cascade button causes all the currently active application windows to overlap so that just the title bars are visible. This way, all windows are accessible.

Tile

If you select the Tile button, the Task Manager will divide the screen among all the active windows. The windows will appear next to one another on the desktop.

Arrange Icons

The Arrange Icons button rearranges the icons in the active window according to the current window size.

Step 10

Printing Files

30

The Print Manager helps you manage the printers that are connected to your system. It also manages the files and documents that you print. All documents printed with a Windows application are routed automatically through the Print Manager, but documents printed with a non-Windows application are not.

Starting the Print Manager

To start the Print Manager, choose its icon from the Main group of the Program Manager. If you have just printed a document from within an application, the Print Manager icon will appear automatically on the lower part of the desktop. In this case, click on the Print Manager icon.

Next, the Print Manager window appears on-screen with the names of the printers that you set up during the installation procedure. Next to the three command buttons, the name of the currently selected printer is displayed. Normally after you call up the Print Manager, the printer is idle.

Printer

Printing with the Print Manager

The Print Manager controls the printer output, but you don't need to call it up to print a file. You must distinguish here between printing documents in Windows and in DOS applications.

Printing in Windows Applications

Because several Windows applications can be active at once, and all of them could theoretically try to access the printer at the same time, Windows applications—unlike DOS applications—don't send data immediately to the printer. Instead, a temporary *spooler file* is produced and given to the Print Manager. The Print Manager lines up the spooler files in a print queue and prints them out as their turns come up. After a spooler file is printed, it is erased.

Print spooler

Printing in Non-Windows Applications

When you are printing a file from a non-Windows application, you cannot start another application until printing is completed. The Print Manager cannot control printing from a non-Windows application. However, you can create a print file with a non-Windows application, and then—back in Windows—have the Print Manager route it to the printer.

Monitoring the Print Queue

When you print from a Windows application, the Print Manager is called up automatically. It appears as a program icon in the lower part of the screen.

Print queue

The Print Manager lists all the files waiting in line in the print queue. The names of the applications that placed print files in the print queue are also listed, as are the names of files that have already been printed. In addition, the Print Manager tells you the size of the print file, what percentage—if any—has already been printed, and where the file is in the queue.

With the View pull-down menu, you can display the date, time, and file size of a document. This information will appear next to its name and that of the application that created it.

Local and Network Print Queues

The Print Manager recognizes two distinct types of print queues—local print queues and network print queues. The local print queue manages files intended for the printer connected directly to your computer. The network print queue manages print files that you intend to print on printers connected to a network.

Controlling the Print Queue

You, as the user, control the local print queue. You can establish a priority for printing files, change the order of the print files, or delete individual entries.

There are two ways to change the order of the print files:

*Changing
the file
order*

- Click on the print file you want to move and hold down the mouse button. A large upward-pointing arrow appears. You can now position the file anywhere you want in the queue.

- Select the print file with the help of the cursor keys and press Ctrl-↑ or Ctrl-↓ to move the file up or down. When you reach the new position, press Enter.

The top print file in the list is currently being printed and so cannot be moved.

To delete a print file, choose the file with the cursor keys or mouse and then select the Delete command button. You will be asked to confirm that you want to delete the file before it is deleted.

*Deleting a
print file*

You can set the "priority"—that is, the print speed—on the Options menu. A high priority means that the other applications are given less CPU time and will run more slowly; a low priority causes printing to run more slowly and the applications to operate more quickly. You must determine where to set the priorities.

*Setting the
print speed*

On the Options menu, you have three options for priority—low, medium, and high. The medium priority option is selected by default.

Leaving the Print Manager

When you close the Print Manager, the print files waiting in the queue will not be printed; they will be removed from the print queue. For this reason, a dialog box appears on the screen to confirm that you really want to leave the Print Manager and not print the leftover files.

*Printing is
interrupted*

Step 11

The PIF Editor

In order to set up and run DOS applications in as problem-free a manner as possible, Windows requires certain information about DOS applications. This information is made available to Windows by way of Program Information Files (PIFs) that are created and used by the PIF Editor.

What Are PIFs?

As you work with Windows 3.1, you must distinguish between applications developed especially for Windows and DOS programs designated by Microsoft as non-Windows applications. Launching a Windows application usually poses no difficulties. Windows can control the program and correctly assess its needs directly from the system resources. DOS applications, however, can cause a serious headache for Windows because many DOS features are adverse to multitasking.

PIFs were created to remedy the situation. PIFs define all the missing but essential information required to make a non-Windows application operate without conflicts. Whenever you start a non-Windows application, Windows searches for a corresponding PIF. If no PIF is found, default settings are used, but these may not be optimal for the program you want to use.

PIFs allow you to run non-Windows applications

When a non-Windows application is operating improperly or if problems occur during or after execution, you should set up a PIF for the application.

During installation, Windows 3.1 sets up PIFs automatically for all the non-Windows applications found on your hard disk drives. Windows 3.1 creates a close-to-optimal PIF at installation time, if it is familiar with the application.

SETUP creates PIFs automatically

Some, but not many, manufacturers deliver their applications with PIFs to ensure that they operate correctly under Windows. When

Copying PIFs

you install an application that you plan to use under Windows, look in the program's documentation and program disks for tips on setting up PIFs. If a PIF is provided, copy it to the Windows directory.

Working with the PIF Editor

Accessories

The PIF Editor, a fixture of Windows 3.1, helps you create and work with PIFs. It is located in the Accessories group. To access the PIF Editor, open the window in the Program Manager and choose the PIF Editor. The application window of the PIF Editor will appear.

Standard and Enhanced mode

The PIF Editor offers two groups of options, depending on whether you want to use Standard or Enhanced mode. The Standard options form the basis of a PIF and are available for both operating modes. The Enhanced options can only be defined when Windows is operating in Enhanced mode.

If you are operating Windows in Standard mode but you want to define the Enhanced options for an application, you must select 386 Enhanced from the Mode menu. You will be asked to confirm your selection. The same is true of Standard mode. If you are currently working in Enhanced mode but you want to define a PIF for operation in Standard mode, you must choose the appropriate mode from the Mode menu.

To operate a non-Windows application, you must specify a number of options and parameters in the PIF. I will discuss these settings later in this Step.

File names

A PIF usually has the same name as its corresponding application, but the file extension .PIF is added. Existing PIFs can be loaded with the File Open menu item.

You should store PIFs in the Windows directory or the directory of the corresponding application. This way, Windows will find the PIF for the application when you call it up (unless you start the application directly from the PIF).

Setting Up and Managing PIFs

With the PIF Editor, you can set up new PIFs for non-Windows applications or edit existing ones. If you want to set up a new PIF, select New from the File menu. Existing PIFs are loaded with the File Open menu item.

When you start a non-Windows application under Windows and the program can't find a corresponding PIF, certain default settings are assumed. These settings are defined in the DEFAULT.PIF file. You can edit this file at any time.

*Default
PIFs*

PIFs for Standard Mode

To define a PIF for use in Standard mode, start Windows 3.1 in Standard mode or choose the mode explicitly from the Mode menu. The entry screen of the PIF Editor is shown in Figure 11.1. Let's look at the various parts of the entry screen. As we do so, you'll see the various tasks that the PIF Editor can accomplish.

In the Program Filename field, the file name of the application is given, including its path and extension.

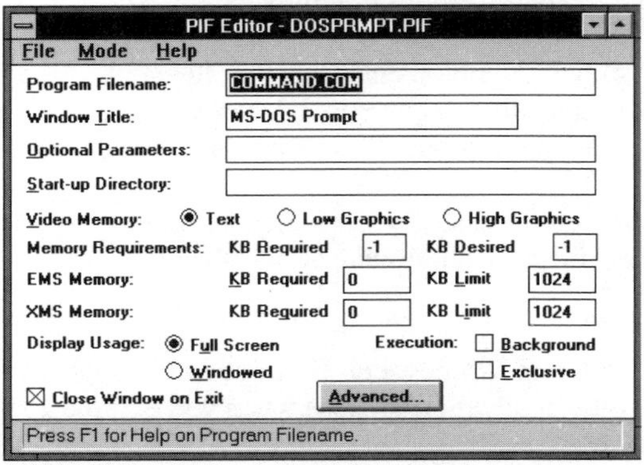

*Program
Filename*

Figure 11.1: Entry screen of the PIF Editor

Windows Title

Windows Title describes the application. This field is optional. If the application is later minimized to icon size, the description will appear below the program icon.

Optional Parameters

The Optional Parameters field defines the program's parameters that are in the command line when you call up the program.

Start-Up Directory

The directory specified in the Start-up Directory will be the default directory when you start the application.

Video Memory

With the Video Memory buttons, you define the video mode to reserve the proper amount of memory: Text for text mode (16K), Low Graphics for CGA graphics (32K), or High Graphics for EGA and VGA graphics (128K).

Memory Require- ments

Specify the minimum and ideal (desired) memory amount that should be available to the application in the Memory Requirements field. If you enter the value −1, all available memory will be put at the application's disposal.

EMS Memory

The EMS Memory field defines the minimum and maximum requirements for expanded memory in kilobytes.

XMS Memory

XMS Memory field defines the minimum and maximum requirements for extended memory in kilobytes.

Display Usage

In the Display Usage box, enter whether the application should be started with the full-screen or in a window. Starting in a window requires more memory but allows for easier data exchange.

Execution

With the Execution option you specify whether the application can be operated in the background or whether it requires the whole computer.

Close Windows on Exit

Activate the Close Windows on Exit option if you want the screen window of the application to close when you exit the application.

Advanced Options of the PIF Editor

To access the additional options of the PIF Editor, choose the Advanced command button. A second page of advanced options appears on the screen. The advanced options are shown in Figure 11.2.

With the advanced options, you define the priorities and the memory requirements of an application for multitasking. To make changes here, you should have a thorough knowledge of multitasking, and you should also be very familiar with the given application. Let's look at the advanced options one at a time.

Priorities

With the Background Priority option you define the relative priority of the process with a value from 0 to 10,000. This value is only considered when Background is selected and Exclusive is not selected.

*Back-
ground
Priority*

The Foreground Priority option lets you define the relative priority of a process with a value from 0 to 10,000 for times when the application is operating in the foreground.

*Fore-
ground
Priority*

```
┌──────────────────────────────────────────────────┐
│              Advanced Options                      │
│ ┌─Multitasking Options─────────────────┐ ┌──────┐ │
│ │ Background Priority: [50]  Foreground │ │  OK  │ │
│ │ Priority: [100]                       │ └──────┘ │
│ │         ⊠ Detect Idle Time            │ ┌──────┐ │
│ │                                       │ │Cancel│ │
│ ┌─Memory Options────────────────────────┐└──────┘ │
│ │  □ EMS Memory Locked    □ XMS Memory Locked     │
│ │  ⊠ Uses High Memory Area □ Lock Application Memory│
│ ┌─Display Options──────────────────────────────────┐
│ │ Monitor Ports:  □ Text  □ Low Graphics □ High Graphics │
│ │       ⊠ Emulate Text Mode  □ Retain Video Memory │
│ ┌─Other Options────────────────────────────────────┐
│ │ ⊠ Allow Fast Paste      □ Allow Close When Active │
│ │ Reserve Shortcut Keys: □ Alt+Tab □ Alt+Esc □ Ctrl+Esc │
│ │                        □ PrtSc  □ Alt+PrtSc □ Alt+Space │
│ │                        □ Alt+Enter               │
│ │ Application Shortcut Key: [None              ]    │
│ └──────────────────────────────────────────────────┘
│ Press F1 for Help on Priority                       │
└──────────────────────────────────────────────────┘
```

Figure 11.2: Advanced options of the PIF Editor

Detect Idle Time

When the Detect Idle Time option is activated, the application turns over its CPU time to other applications when it is idle—for example, when it is waiting for user input.

Memory Options

With EMS Memory Locked and XMS Memory Locked, you can prevent Windows from swapping expanded (EMS) and extended (XMS) memory to the hard disk. This accelerates the process but reduces the overall performance.

The Uses High Memory Area option specifies whether the application may make use of the first 64K of extended memory (HMA).

The Lock Application Memory option lets you specify that the working memory (RAM) of the application never be swapped to the hard disk. This accelerates the process but reduces the overall performance.

Display Options

With the Display Options, you tell the application how to operate with the graphics card. Setting these options is especially important if the application accesses the graphics card directly. Here, you define the screen mode used. Try other settings if using the application causes problems. With the Retain Video Memory, you tell Windows not to swap video memory to the hard disk.

Other Options

Use the Other Options to reserve key combinations that have a special meaning under Windows but are used as well by the DOS application.

The Allow Fast Paste option allows Windows to transfer data in the quickest possible mode to the application from the Clipboard. Deactivate this option if you have difficulties during data exchange.

The Allow Close When Active option allows you to exit an application even if it wasn't exited properly. With DOS applications it is better not to use this option.

Application Shortcut Key

The Application Shortcut Key option lets you define the key combination—with Alt, Ctrl, or Shift—that brings the application to the foreground.

Leaving the PIF Editor

Before you leave the PIF Editor, make sure you have saved the modified PIF under the file name you intended and that your file is in the correct directory. Next, select Exit from the File pull-down menu.

Step 12

Exchanging Application Data

Windows' intuitive graphical user interface and its multitasking capabilities are two of the program's outstanding advantages—but by no means are they the only ones. The various ways to comfortably and easily exchange data between applications are often overlooked. In this step I will introduce various techniques for exchanging data.

Techniques for Exchanging Data

Windows 3.1 provides you with three techniques for exchanging data between Windows applications: the Clipboard, DDE, and OLE. The three are similar and complement each other quite well.

The Clipboard

The Clipboard is a temporary holding place for one-time data exchanges between two applications. For example, if you wanted to copy a text or modify part of a picture, you could use the Clipboard. You select the section of the document you want to copy, copy it to the Clipboard, and transfer it (via the Clipboard) to the target application. It doesn't matter whether you are copying text or pictures because the Clipboard can work with diverse formats.

Use the Clipboard for one-time exchanges

You access the Clipboard's functions from the Edit pull-down menu of almost all Windows applications. Here you can copy, cut, or paste a portion of data.

Dynamic Data Exchange

Dynamic Data Exchange (DDE) is the second way to exchange data under Windows. With DDE, you create links between different types of data objects. For example, if you listed the price of various products in advertising copy, and you modified the price in

DDE

a spreadsheet, it would be great if that change could be made automatically in the advertising copy whenever the spreadsheet changed. Science fiction? Hardly—this is DDE.

DDE is possible under Windows only when the applications involved support dynamic data exchange. Unfortunately, not all Windows applications support DDE. Read the manuals provided with your applications to see if they offer DDE capabilities. Professional applications such as Microsoft Excel and AutoCAD support DDE as a matter of course.

Object Linking and Embedding

OLE

Object Linking and Embedding (OLE) is a newly developed technique that allows flexible—and, more importantly, dynamic—links between documents. OLE is helping to realize Bill Gates's dream of "information at your fingertips."

The Clipboard and DDE remain the established ways of exchanging data under Windows, however. OLE should not replace these methods, but supplement them. You don't always need to establish a link between two applications—sometimes you just need to copy data. If this is the case, use the Clipboard.

Embedding and Linking

OLE provides two ways to transfer information. Either you "embed" the information in your target document—a technique comparable to operating with the Clipboard—or you maintain a more lasting connection, or link, between the target document and the source of the information (which is recognized by DDE applications). An "embedded" piece of information doesn't change. On the other hand, when you create a link, the information is always updated from the document the information was taken from.

How the Techniques Differ

Source unknown

The difference between information transferred from the Clipboard and information embedded with OLE is that, with the Clipboard, embedded information is anonymous and no one knows where it came from. Information transferred via OLE, like information transferred with the Clipboard, is static, but the source of the information is known.

Both DDE and OLE are dynamic, but only with OLE objects can you automatically start the concealed application—that is, the application used to create the object in the first place—by double-clicking on the object. For example, if a Write document contained an object created by Paintbrush, you could open Paintbrush automatically to modify the object by simply pointing with the mouse and double-clicking on the object.

Difference between DDE and OLE

Working with the Clipboard

You can transfer only one object with the Clipboard. It can be text, a picture, or a spreadsheet—the data format doesn't matter. Data that has been transferred to the Clipboard doesn't have to be worked on immediately. It can be stored in a Clipboard file, on a floppy disk, or on a hard disk.

Data stored on the Clipboard remains there until you delete it or overwrite it with new data. Windows doesn't display a warning to keep data from being overwritten on the Clipboard.

Copying Data to the Clipboard

There are several ways to copy data to the Clipboard. Each Windows application offers a menu option for copying part of a document to the Clipboard. With non-Windows applications, you can only copy text to the Clipboard.

To exchange data by way of the Clipboard, proceed step-by-step as follows:

Copying part of a document

1. Select the text or graphic section that you want to copy to the Clipboard.

2. Select Copy or Cut from the Edit pull-down menu to move the marked block to the Clipboard.

- With Cut, the marked block is copied to the Clipboard and removed from the source document.

- With Copy, the marked block remains intact in the source document.

3. Select the application in which you want to work with the data you copied to the Clipboard.

4. Position the cursor where you want to insert the data.

5. Select Paste from the Edit pull-down menu. With some applications, such as Paintbrush, you must then place the object manually.

Copying
the screen
contents

To copy the contents of a screen to the Clipboard, press the PrtScr key. Windows will copy the screen contents to the Clipboard as a bitmap. Graphics applications such as Paintbrush can then read in the screen contents easily.

To copy only the application window or a dialog box, just press Alt-PrtScr.

Working with OLE

How you link objects with OLE depends heavily on the application's capabilities and how the application functions. Study the manual for your installed software before you use OLE.

To fully utilize the capabilities of OLE, you most often use the Edit pull-down menu, as with the Clipboard. This menu offers more ways to embed objects in your document or create a link.

Embedding Objects

An embedded object is stored with the document. The link connects it to the application that produced it. To embed an object in a document—for example a graphic in a Write document—proceed as follows:

1. Select Insert Object from the Edit pull-down menu.

2. Select the object type. For our example, select Paintbrush Picture.

3. Paintbrush is started. You can now proceed as you like, by creating a picture or loading an existing one from the hard disk.

4. Select Exit from the File pull-down menu and confirm the action. The object will appear in the text document.

Now, by double-clicking on the object or by selecting Edit Object, you can work on the Paintbrush object whenever you like. Write will know to start Paintbrush accordingly.

Creating Links

When you create a link, the object is not stored in the document: a pointer to the corresponding file is. For example, if you have a drawing DOG.PCX and you create a link to this object, DOG.PCX will be displayed in your document and modifications to the file will be immediately visible.

As an example, the following procedure links a graphic to a Write document:

1. Start the application with which you want to create a link, such as Paintbrush.

2. Load the document with which you want to establish a link or create a new drawing. Save your graphic under a new file name.

3. Select the section that you want to use in your text document.

4. Choose Copy from the Edit pull-down menu.

5. Switch to the Write word processor.

6. Position the cursor and choose Paste Link.

The object appears in the text document and can be modified at any time by either modifying the original Paintbrush file or by double-clicking on the object from within Write.

Any time you open a file that contains a link to another file, the application asks if you want to update the link. If you want to include the latest version of the linked object, click on Yes.

Windows 3.1 employs a new technology for representing fonts on the screen and sending them to the printer. The name of this new technique is TrueType. It was developed cooperatively by Microsoft and Apple, by the way.

While a large amount of modern technology is behind TrueType, that doesn't necessarily mean more work for the user. On the contrary, after you have installed Windows 3.1 on your computer, the fourteen new TrueType fonts are immediately available to you. All Bitmap fonts from Windows 3.0 are still available as well.

The New TrueType Fonts

I mentioned fourteen fonts. In reality, there are three font families with four styles each, and two fonts that only offer one style. The following TrueType fonts are offered under Windows 3.1:

- Arial
- Courier New
- Times New Roman
- Symbol
- WingDing

The TrueType fonts

The first three fonts—Arial, Courier New, and Times New Roman—are offered in four styles: normal, bold, italic, and bold italic. These font-styles are not derived (one could easily derive the bold or italic presentation from a normal font), but are available as separate font files in order to improve their quality. The thirteenth and fourteenth fonts, Symbol and WingDing, are not available in bold, italic, or bold italic.

Different styles

Using Fonts in Applications

Because it is advantageous to use TrueType fonts wherever possible, you need to know how to distinguish them from Bitmap fonts. One way to distinguish them would be to keep track of the font names, but that would get wearisome after a while, especially if you were to install more TrueType fonts. Fortunately, Windows provides a much simpler way to distinguish TrueType from Bitmap fonts. Whenever you choose a font, you can tell immediately whether it's a Bitmap or TrueType font. Try it out:

1. Start the Write word processor and type in a few characters.

2. Choose Fonts from the Character pull-down menu.

3. A dialog box appears like the one in Figure 13.1. Here, all fonts that are currently installed under Windows are displayed.

In front of each font name, in most cases, is a little icon. This icon tells you whether the font is a printer font or a TrueType font. TrueType fonts are preceded by the pair of letters "TT". Printer fonts, which are only intended for a given printer, are preceded by a small printer icon.

Whichever font you select, some example letters appear in the sample window. They appear in the font size you selected. When

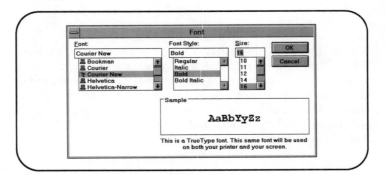

Figure 13.1: Selecting fonts is very easy.

you select a TrueType font, a note appears below the window informing you that the font you selected will be used both as a screen font and as a printer font.

When you choose a Bitmap font, a note appears advising you that it is a printer font and that what you see on the screen will not correspond exactly to the font that is printed. Windows selects as comparable a font as possible for screen display. The same goes for screen fonts. Windows selects as near as possible a font to the one that will be printed.

Not all Windows applications offer this service when you select fonts. Only those applications delivered with Windows 3.1 and some especially modern applications such as Excel 4.0 and Word for Windows 2.0 try to approximate screen and printer fonts—all others will certainly follow suit.

Managing Fonts

To manage the fonts available in the system, use the Fonts menu item in the Control Panel. Once you select Fonts, you have access to all the currently installed fonts and can also install new fonts.

The Control Panel displays all installed fonts in alphabetical order. After the name of the font, the type sizes that are available to it are displayed. With TrueType fonts, this is superfluous, since TrueType fonts can be drawn in any size. With all other fonts, the type size and in some cases the characteristics (such as Super VGA or 8514/A) are displayed.

Delete the fonts that you never work with to save space on your hard disk. To delete a font:

Deleting a font

1. Start the Control Panel and select the Fonts entry.

2. Mark the unwanted font and select the Delete command.

3. A warning appears asking if you really want to delete the font. You can also choose to remove the font from the list or actually erase the font file.

Be careful with the Yes to All command button, since you can accidentally delete font files you really want. The same goes for the Delete Font File From Disk option.

Adding a font

To bring either TrueType or a Bitmap font into the system, proceed as follows:

1. Start the Control Panel and select the Fonts entry.

2. Select the Add command button. A list of fonts that are present on the hard disk, but not yet installed, appears on the screen.

3. If you want to install the fonts to an optional font disk, insert the font disk in the floppy disk drive and enter the drive letter for the drive. For example, you could enter **A:**.

4. Fonts that can be installed in Windows appear in the List of Fonts. Choose the ones you wish to install or select them all with the Select All menu item.

After confirming the selected fonts, the Control Panel installs them. Distinguishing between TrueType and other types of fonts is not necessary here.

If you try to select a font that is already present, an error message appears. You can't overwrite an existing font. In order to do so, you must delete the existing font (preferably with the option that also removes the font file), and then reinstall the appropriate one.

TrueType Options

Using TrueType fonts

After you have selected Fonts in the Control Panel, a dialog box appears with the installed fonts. Next to familiar command buttons like Cancel, Delete and Add, you will find another command button called "TrueType."

Click the TrueType command button and the options appear for managing the TrueType fonts. With the first option, Enable TrueType Fonts, you determine whether to use the True Type fonts at all. If for some reason you don't want to use TrueType fonts, deactivate the check box.

If you attempt to change the Enable TrueType Fonts setting, a dialog box appears. It tells you that changing this setting will only take effect when you next restart Windows. You can now decide whether you want to continue working in Windows as before (No Restart), or whether you want to restart Windows in order for the changes to take effect.

Restart
required

Using TrueType Fonts Exclusively

You can also determine whether to display TrueType fonts exclusively in the TrueType options dialog box. Making only TrueType fonts available in Windows applications is a good way to prevent printer and screen fonts from accidentally being used.

Printing TrueType Fonts

An aesthetically pleasing font on the screen is very fine, but more to the point is making sure that the output of the printer is of equally good quality. This way WYSIWYG ("What You See Is What You Get") becomes a reality.

Dot-matrix printers in general don't have TrueType capability. The printout from Windows must come as a graphic bitmap. With some printers, you can define individual fonts. Windows understands this and defines the required fonts during printing.

Dot-matrix
printers

With laser printers, the procedure is usually different. With a PCL printer—this class includes the HP printers and their compatibles—the required fonts are loaded into the printer as bitmap fonts. To keep the loading procedure from taking too long, only the required characters are loaded. This takes less time than loading an entire font. Loading only the required characters is even possible on an HP LaserJet, which normally doesn't allow the downloading of character sets.

Laser
printers

PostScript
printers

Finally, with PostScript printers, the required TrueType fonts are also loaded—a procedure that takes no more time than loading PostScript fonts. (It's even possible to use the built-in PostScript fonts and to display analogous TrueType fonts on the screen.) The output of TrueType fonts on PostScript printers is reliable and fast.

TrueImage
printers

The most optimal performance comes, of course, from TrueImage printers that have internal TrueType fonts. With TrueImage printers, converting the character sets is no longer required because Windows and the printer speak the same language. At this time, however, few TrueImage printers are available.

Overview of Multimedia

With Windows 3.1, the age of multimedia has definitely arrived. You can play music under Windows, reproduce speech, edit video, and do much more—that is, if you have the right hardware. And whether you do or not, Windows 3.1 prepares you and your computer for the PC's new uses.

The new capabilities of Windows 3.1 are made possible through multimedia Application Program Interfaces (APIs). APIs are functions internal to Windows. They serve to manage video and sound. They are and will be incorporated into all Windows versions from now on. This fact is of great significance to program developers.

APIs

The Sound Recorder in particular, and the Media Player as well—both found in the Accessories program group—are the two most prevalent multimedia tools found in Windows 3.1. But the Control Panel has also been expanded to offer multimedia capabilities.

The Media Player

With the Media Player, an entirely new Windows application, you can play multimedia files. Examples of multimedia files include files with acoustic contents, such as files that contain sound data in the MIDI standard. Recorded sound can also be played back. You could produce the squeaking of a door or reproduce a speech by John F. Kennedy.

If they're available, you can also display video sequences from CD-ROM or video discs on the screen. Working with sound data is possible today.

Video

However, to produce sound your computer must have the right hardware. It must have a soundboard that meets the requirements of the MPC standard. If you don't have this hardware, don't bother trying to run the Media Player.

The Sound Recorder

You can create or modify files that contain digitized sound data with the Sound Recorder. Such files have the file extension .WAV (Wave). When Wave files are played by the Sound Recorder or the Media Player, what you hear sounds like a stereo system. The Sound Recorder is shown in Figure 14.1.

Memory-intensive

In principle, there are no limits to the quality of sound files. Sound files are, however, very memory-intensive. As little as two or three seconds of sound can use more than 100K.

Recording

You can record sound data and store it in Wave files. For example, you can speak into a microphone and transfer your voice to an application such as Microsoft Excel. (From there, you can play it when needed, an innovation made possible by OLE.) You can also modify other audio signals, such as those from stereo systems. Think of the Sound Recorder as a type of sound editor. Not a professional one, of course, but it's a beginning.

Enhancements to the Control Panel

To control the functions connected with multimedia, the Control Panel was enhanced to make some additional capabilities available.

Drivers

With the help of Drivers, which are shown in Figure 14.2, you can control the required drivers and install them in your system (you don't use SETUP to control multimedia device drivers). Later, if

Figure 14.1: The Sound Recorder modifies sound files.

you connect a video disc player to your computer, you install the
corresponding device driver with Drivers.

Windows is already outfitted with device drivers for the most
important soundboards like Soundblaster from Creative Labs and
the Thunder Board from Media Vision. If you have a soundboard,
activate the corresponding device driver in this way:

1. Start the Control Panel.

2. Select Drivers.

3. Select the Add entry.

4. If the name of your soundboard appears in the list, select it
   and confirm by clicking OK.

5. Select Close.

6. Drivers probably will ask you to insert a diskette. Insert the
   diskette and confirm.

Follow the same procedure to install additional soundboards that
conform to the MPC standard.

Pay careful attention to the instructions in the multimedia hardware
manuals.

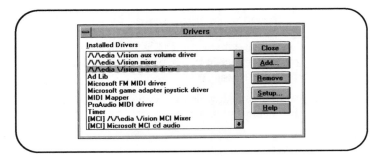

Figure 14.2: Device drivers controlled with Drivers

The MIDI Standard and the MIDI Mapper

MIDI Mapper

In order to support the MIDI capabilities of a soundboard, the MIDI Mapper is required. The MIDI Mapper is only accessible if you have a sound card installed. You load and modify various different MIDI tables with the MIDI Mapper, which is shown in Figure 14.3. The currently active MIDI table is responsible for how the MIDI sound file sounds when it is played.

Managing Sound Files

Sound

Finally, with the help of the expanded Sounds entries in the Control Panel, you can not only decide whether acoustic signals are supported under Windows, but also which ones are supported.

Assigning sounds

As long as a soundboard is installed in your computer and it is supported by Windows, you can assign certain Wave files to specific events. This way, a special sound file can play when you start Windows, exit Windows, or when an error occurs. To assign a Wave File to a specific event:

1. Start the Control Panel.

2. Select Sounds. A dialog box like the one in Figure 14.4 appears.

3. In the left field, labeled "Events," select the event you want to assign the sound to.

4. In the right field, labeled "Files," select the sound file you want to be played when the event takes place. It must be a file with the extension .WAV.

    • If you want to hear what the file sounds like first, press the Test command button.

5. Confirm your selection with OK or void all of the definitions with Cancel.

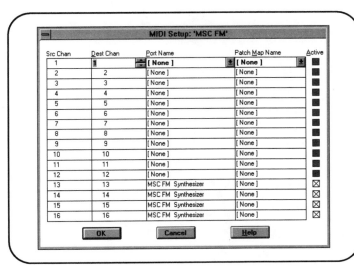

Figure 14.3: The MIDI Mapper

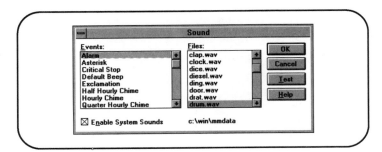

Figure 14.4: New sound possibilities offered by Windows 3.1

Step 15

The Control Panel

The graphical user interface of Windows 3.1 is very flexible. You can customize it for your needs in many ways. While you can control some parts of Windows with the SETUP program, the Control Panel passes on your personal requirements to the graphical user interface.

Starting the Control Panel

The Control Panel is represented by a program icon of the same name in the Main group. To control the manner in which Windows 3.1 operates, select the Control Panel icon. The Control Panel's functions are offered in a special window. We will go over its functions in this Step.

Unlike Windows 3.0, the contents as well as the size of the window can be altered in Windows 3.1. Besides changing the size and form of the window, you can expand the functions of the Control Panel to accommodate Windows' multimedia components.

Colors

With the Colors option, you can control the screen colors that Windows displays. When you select Colors, a window appears displaying the most important parts of the Windows 3.1 screen. In the Color Schemes list box, you can choose from 23 default color combinations for your Windows 3.1 screen.

Default color combina-tions

When you select the Color Palette option, a color palette appears on the screen. Besides the default colors you have at your disposal, you can define up to 16 custom colors—depending on your monitor type. In the Screen Element list box you'll find all the recognizable elements, including Desktop, Window Background, and Menu Text. You can assign new colors to each of these elements individually.

Editing the color palette

Select the Define Custom Colors command button to define a color other than the ones displayed in the Basic Colors. Depending on

Defining a new color

which video card you installed in your computer, different degrees of color shading are available. With a VGA card, you can select nearly as many colors as you want. Figure 15.1 shows the Custom Color Selector for a VGA card.

Adding colors

Under Custom Colors, you select the field for the color you wish to define. You can select any color in the color field with the mouse. Once you've selected a color, confirm your choice by clicking on Add Color.

End the procedure by clicking the Close button. Next, confirm the new color palette by clicking OK or by pressing Enter.

Fonts

Under Fonts, you define which typestyles are available and how they should be dealt with. You'll find a thorough description of fonts in Step 13.

Ports

With Ports, you can set the parameters of the serial ports installed in your system.

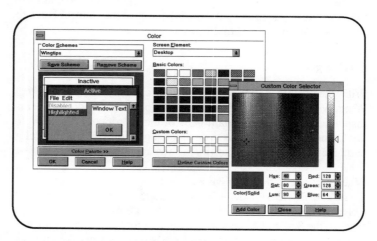

Figure 15.1: An extensive color palette

Mouse

With the Mouse icon, you define how fast the mouse pointer should track and how quickly the mouse button must be pressed twice in order to complete a double-click. You can also make either the left or the right mouse button the action key. By default, the left button is the action key, but you can select the right button if you want to—an option often taken by left-handed people. In the test field, you can see the blink rate or try out the double-clicking interval.

Double-click

Desktop

Under Desktop, you control the elements of the Windows Desktop. You can specify the background pattern, the cursor blink rate, and the icon spacing.

You can select a special background pattern. Thirteen standard patterns are shipped with Windows 3.1. You can also designate a pattern of your own. To designate a standard pattern or define a new one, select the Edit Pattern button. Give the pattern a new name and select Add.

Back-ground patterns

Applications

Switching through applications is much faster with Alt-Tab than with Alt-Esc. When the new Fast "Alt+Tab" Switching option is active, Alt-Tab operates even more quickly because only the application's name and icon appear in the center of the screen. By letting go of the Alt key, you can bring the displayed application to the foreground.

Screen Saver

Windows 3.1 offers screen savers to prevent "burn-in" on the monitor. Burn-in occurs when a computer is idle and a picture remains on the screen for a long period of time. A screen saver shuts down the screen automatically when a certain time has elapsed without any keyboard activity or mouse movements. To select a screen saver, proceed as follows:

1. Start the Control Panel and select Desktop.

2. Click on Screen Saver Name.

3. Select the screen saver with the mouse or cursor keys.

   - You can see the screen saver in action with the Test option. When you move the mouse or press a key, the computer continues working.

4. Configure the current screen saver under Setup. Here you tell Windows how many figures should appear or what the text should be.

5. Under Delay, define how many minutes without mouse movement or keyboard activity should elapse before the screen saver is activated.

Wallpaper

Any bitmap file—that is, a file with the extension .BMP—can function as a background for the desktop. Figure 15.2 shows an example of a new backgroud. The bitmap file need only be present in the Windows working directory (usually C:\WINDOWS) for you to access it. Proceed as follows to assign a new background to the desktop:

*Assigning
a new
back-
ground*

1. Start the Control Panel and select Desktop.

2. Select a file from the Wallpaper file list box. Use the ↓ key or the mouse to make the selection.

3. Select Center or Tile.

   - With Center, the picture is centered on the screen.

   - With Tile, the picture fills the screen.

*Icon
Spacing*

Under Icon Spacing, you define the distance between two icons in the Program Manager. The distance is measured in pixels. The pixel value is normally calculated automatically, but can be changed if certain icons overlap.

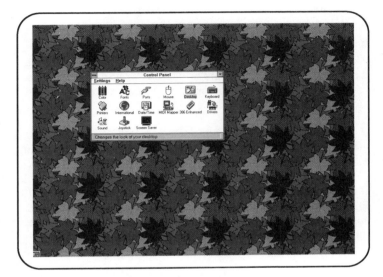

Figure 15.2: A bitmap file as Wallpaper for the desktop

To position a window, Windows 3.1 lays invisible lines in a grid on the screen. With Granularity you define the distance between these invisible lines. Normally, windows can be moved without being forced into coordinates set at specific intervals. All values between 0 and 45 are possible.

Granul-arity

With Border Width, you specify how wide to make window frames. The bigger the frame, the larger the area you can select to change the window's dimensions. The width you specify here applies to all resizable windows. Any value between 1 and 49 is possible, but only values between 2 and 7 are advised.

Border Width

Under Cursor Blink Rate, you define the blinking frequency of the screen cursor. You can choose a relative value between Slow and Fast. A sample cursor shows the blinking rate.

Cursor Blink Rate

Under Keyboard, you define the key repeat rate of the keyboard on a relative scale. In a second field, you can try out the key repeat rate.

Keyboard

Printers

Windows 3.1 works with nearly all commercially available printers. With Printers, you can install additional printers as you require them. However, to install more printers, you must have the appropriate Windows 3.1 program diskettes (or the driver diskette provided by the printer manufacturer).

If you've installed more than one active printer, you can make one the default. You can also specify the port and its corresponding transmission parameters.

Print Manager

If you don't want to print with the Print Manager, deactivate the Use Print Manager check box. If you do so, the printer output of the application will be sent directly to the printer—it will not be routed through the Print Manager.

International

Country code and time format

Under International, you can define the country code for Windows in general as well as all Windows applications. When you choose a country code, you automatically adopt the time and date formats of the country you chose. However, you can also configure these default settings separately if you want to.

Date/Time

The Date/Time option allows you to set the current system date and time. You can either enter the values from the keyboard, or increase or decrease the values in single unit increments with the mouse.

386 Enhanced

80386 or higher

If you are running Windows 3.1 on a computer with an 80386 or higher and you are using Enhanced mode, you will find an additional icon on the Control Panel: 386 Enhanced. With this function you can more closely control the division of CPU time to the various applications and peripheral devices.

Warning

In Enhanced mode, several DOS applications can be active at once, and in theory all of them may simultaneously try to access the same system resources and ports. Under Device Contention, you can tell Windows what to do when such an event occurs. As a rule, it is best to have a warning appear. To make a warning appear, choose the Always Warn option.

Virtual Memory

New to Windows 3.1 is the ability to define the size and type of virtual memory directly from the Control Panel without having to hunt for the SWAPFILE application. Because virtual memory is only available in Enhanced mode, it makes sense to put this option under the 386 Enhanced category. A description of how to work with virtual memory appears in Step 20.

Virtual memory

Sound

With Sound, you can tell Windows when to issue audio signals. An error beep is an example of an audio signal. If your computer doesn't have a soundboard, the only acoustic signal it can manage is a beep. With Enable System Sounds, you can determine whether acoustic signals are supported.

If a soundboard is installed in your computer, many more possiblities are available to you. These are described in Step 14.

When you installed Windows with the SETUP program, you told Windows about your individual preferences and hard- and software components. In other words, you *configured* Windows 3.1.

However, if you make changes afterward to your hardware or software configuration—for example, if you install a new graphics card—you may have to configure Windows again. With SETUP, you have access to the current configuration and can make changes to the configuration as well.

Starting SETUP

After you install Windows, the SETUP installation program is transformed into a configuration program. SETUP is available at any time from the Main group of the Program Manager.

To check the current configuration of Windows and see if changes have occurred in your computer's configuration, start SETUP. To do this, open the Main group and click on Windows Setup.

SETUP opens an application window. From here, you can

- view and modify the current configuration of Windows 3.1,

or

- search through the hard disk drives for standard applications and install them in the appropriate program groups.

Working with SETUP

When you start SETUP, Windows checks the system configuration. It displays information about the system (but not as exhaustively as it does during the installation procedure), as shown in Figure 16.1.

Changing the System Configuration

To change the system settings, select Change System Settings from the Options menu. You can change the following settings:

- the video adapter type
- the mouse type
- the keyboard type
- the network type

To change one of the displayed values, select its list box with the mouse or the Tab key, as shown in Figure 16.2. Next, select a value from the list, again using either the mouse or keyboard.

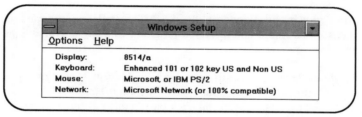

Figure 16.1: SETUP displays information about the current system configuration.

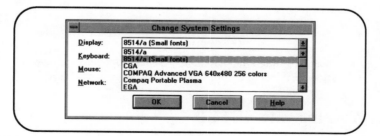

Figure 16.2: Changing the configuration with SETUP

When you select the new entries, you sometimes must insert an installation diskette so that SETUP can copy the necessary files and configure the system to incorporate the changes.

Restart the system after you make changes to the system settings. By leaving Windows 3.1 and starting it again, you make sure the changes are in effect.

Installing Applications

When you installed Windows 3.1, you had the program search the hard disk for existing applications. SETUP collected the programs in the Applications program group.

If you installed new software packages since you installed Windows or if you put off searching the hard disk during the Windows installation procedure, you can still make the search. SETUP can search your drives for applications and set them up to run with Windows. Follow this procedure:

1. Select Setup Applications from the Options menu.

2. Select Search for applications.

3. Tell Windows where to look for the applications, as shown in Figure 16.3. By clicking with the mouse, mark

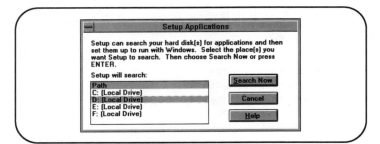

Figure 16.3: Searching for applications with SETUP

which hard disk drives should be searched. The entry PATH shows the current search path.

4. Choose Search Now. SETUP begins the search.

SETUP doesn't locate all applications, of course, but it will find all Windows applications and all common DOS applications.

5. You can install all the applications permanently or install selected ones. Mark the applications you want to install in the left window and click Add->. If you are using the keyboard, choose applications with the cursor keys, and mark files with the spacebar.

6. Confirm the installation with OK. SETUP will add the programs you selected to the Applications program group.

If you want to copy all the applications listed in the left window to the right window, and in so doing install them as well under the Program Manager, click on Add All.

Applications accidentally copied into the right window can be marked and copied back into the left window with <-Remove.

Adding or Removing Windows Components

The Add/Remove Windows Components menu item is new to Windows 3.1. With it, you can add or remove individual Windows program files. Windows components that you don't use often can be removed to conserve disk space.

Gaining
storage
capacity

If, for example, you never make use of the Solitaire or Minesweeper games, you can remove them with a few keystrokes and create 240K of additional disk space at the same time.

When you select Add/Remove Windows Components, a dialog box appears, as shown in Figure 16.4. This dialog box displays the various components. You can now activate or deactivate a component by clicking on its check box. To activate or deactivate files within a component, press the adjoining Files button. Instead of

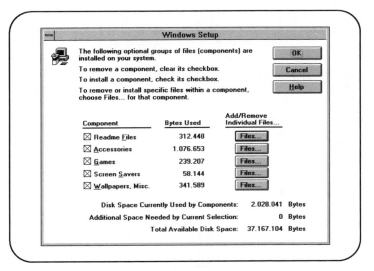

Figure 16.4: Removing or installing Windows components

meaningless file names, brief descriptions appear, along with the number of bytes required for each component.

Starting SETUP from DOS

If you need to install a device driver that is required to work with Windows—such as a device driver for a video card—you must start the SETUP program from DOS because in such cases you can't even load Windows.

After you have made the required changes to your computer, turn your computer on and start the SETUP program by entering

    SETUP

You can also change individual system components. Beyond that, you can install third-party device drivers, such as those for graphics cards.

Leaving
SETUP

To end your work with SETUP, choose Exit from the Options pull-down menu. You can also close SETUP via the Control menu, of course.

When you leave SETUP, the modifications are made to the system. A dialog box appears, allowing you to restart Windows now. This is advisable, because by leaving the system and restarting you make sure your changes are in effect.

The Write Word Processor

Microsoft's Write word processor comes as standard equipment with Windows 3.1. With Write, you can produce business letters simply and easily, and even create demanding page layouts.

Working with Write

You'll find Write in the Accessories group. To start Write, select Accessories from the Program Manager and then start Write. Write is the first application in the group.

Starting Write

After you start Write, the program opens a document window. Write can modify only one document at a time. You cannot open several documents in different document windows and work on them all at the same time.

In the text area of the Write window you will see up to three distinct symbols—the insertion point, mouse pointer, and end mark. They are shown in Figure 17.1.

The *insertion point* marks the cursor position where characters will be inserted when you start typing.

Elements of a Write screen

With the *mouse pointer*, you can move to any place in the text or mark a block of text.

The *end mark* indicates the end of the document. No editing operations are possible past this point.

The *page status area* shows which page is currently being displayed. Here, you'll see a value of 2 once you pass the first page break.

You can begin entering text immediately after starting the program. Characters entered with the keyboard appear at the insertion point. Write breaks lines automatically, based on the current paragraph and character settings. To end a paragraph, press Enter.

Entering text

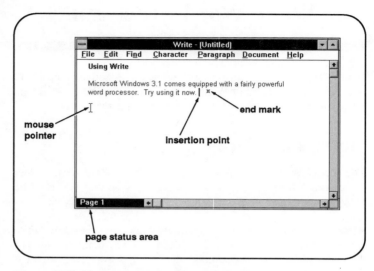

Figure 17.1: Elements of the Write word processor

Positioning the inser- tion point

There are several ways to position the insertion point. Of course, you can move the insertion point with the cursor keys or mouse pointer anywhere in the text.

If you are working with the keyboard, you can move the insertion point with various key combinations similar to those found in other word processors. Write also offers key combinations with the Goto key. The Goto key is the 5 key on the numeric keypad, a key not normally used. To use the 5 key as a Goto key, you must have Num Lock turned off. Table 17.1 shows key commands for moving the insertion point in Write.

Moving the insertion point

Keys	Moves to
End	End of the line
Home	Beginning of the line
Ctrl-→	Next word

Table 17.1: Key Functions for Cursor Movement

Keys	Moves to
Ctrl-←	Previous word
Ctrl-End	End of the document
Ctrl-PgDn	Bottom of the window
Ctrl-PgUp	Top of the window
Ctrl-Home	Beginning of the document
Goto-↑	Previous paragraph
Goto-↓	Next paragraph
Goto-→	Next sentence
Goto-←	Previous sentence
Goto-PgDn	Next page
Goto-PgUp	Previous page

Table 17.1: Key Functions for Cursor Movement (continued)

Going to another page with the Goto-PgUp or Goto-PgDn key combinations is only possible if you've already created a page break in the text.

Selecting a Text Passage

For many commands, you have to select a section of text. You can do this with the mouse by moving to the beginning of the text, holding down the button, moving the mouse to the end of the text, and releasing the mouse button.

You can also select text a word at a time instead of a character at a time. To select text word by word, double-click on the first word, hold down the mouse button, and drag the mouse to the end of the text.

Selecting words

Finally, you can select text line by line or paragraph by paragraph. To select text line by line, move the mouse pointer to the selection

Selecting lines

area located to the left of the text area. The mouse pointer changes from an I-beam to an arrow. Now, click the mouse button. The current line is selected. By holding the button down and dragging the mouse, you can select an entire text passage. To select text paragraph by paragraph, move the mouse pointer into the selection area and double-click. Now you can select text paragraph by paragraph. Table 17.2 gives a summary of how to select text passages with Write.

To Select	*Action*
characters	Click and move in the text area
words	Double-click and move in the text area
lines	Click and move in the selection area
paragraphs	Double-click and move in the selection area

Table 17.2: Mouse Movements for Selecting Text

Finding and Replacing Text

You can find and also replace text with Write. The find and/or replace procedure always begins at the current position of the insertion point. To find and replace text:

1. Click on the Find menu option.

2. Click on Replace. A dialog box appears.

3. Enter the text string that you want to find, as in Figure 17.2.

4. As the second parameter, enter the replacement text. Neither the find nor the replace entry can be longer than 255 characters.

   • Select the Match Whole Word Only check box if you want the text replaced only if it stands by itself and is not part of another word. For example, if you were changing "the" to "a" you would select Match Whole Word Only. If you didn't, the word "another" would change to "anoaer."

- Normally, Write ignores whether the text is upper- or lowercase. If you want the program to consider case, activate the Match Case check box.

There are three replacement command buttons:

Find Next   Finds the next entry and shows its position in the text. You can also press F3 to activate this command.

Replace   Replaces the currently selected text with the replacement text string.

Replace All   Replaces all instances of the Find text after the cursor position with the Replace With text.

If you ever want to search for the next occurrence of the text, you can select the Find Next key (F3).

The windows of the Replace dialog box remain on-screen during search-and-replace procedures. This way, the command buttons are always available. If you want to end an action, you must close the corresponding window via the Control menu. You can have both a find and a replace window open simultaneously.

Use the wildcard replacement characters shown in Table 17.3 in the Find What text box for maximum flexibility.

Wildcard characters

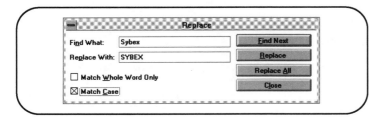

Figure 17.2: Finding and replacing a text passage

Wildcard	Meaning
?	Placeholder for any character
^w	Placeholder for a blank space
^t	Tab character
^p	Paragraph mark
^d	Manual page break

Table 17.3: Wildcards for Finding and Replacing Text

Write Files

By default, Write works with files that have the extension .WRI, but it can also read foreign formats, including text documents from Word for DOS and normal text files (without special formatting characters). If you select a foreign file, Write asks if you want to convert it to Write format.

Formatting

Of course, you can format the text any way you like by using various fonts, styles, and sizes. These options are available from the Character pull-down menu. You have the most options when you activate the Fonts menu item.

Once you pull down the character menu, Write offers you a dialog box with many different possibilities. You can select any available font. A font sample is displayed for whichever font you select.

Leaving Write

To end your work with Write, select Exit from the File pull-down menu. If you've made modifications to the current document, you will be told as much. You then have the option of saving the changes before you exit Write for good.

Step 18

Working with Paintbrush

Paintbrush is a painting and drawing program that's easy to use and a standard accessory to Windows 3.1. It allows you to create colorful bitmap graphics. However, the program has many features and all of them can't be covered here. In this step, you'll find general tips for operating Paintbrush.

Starting Paintbrush

Paintbrush is a part of the Accessories group. To start the Paintbrush program, select the Accessories group from the Program Manager. Next, select the Paintbrush program icon, which is represented by an artist's palette and brush.

In Paintbrush, you can only edit one document at a time. So when you start Paintbrush, expand the application window. Some screen components, such as the command icons in the left panel, are hard to read in a small application window.

Using Paintbrush

It is much easier to use Paintbrush with the mouse than with the keyboard. However, if you prefer to use the keyboard, shortcut keys available to you are summarized in Table 18.1.

Key	*Mouse Equivalent*
Insert	Clicking or pressing the left mouse button
Delete	Clicking or pressing the right mouse button
F9-Insert	Double-clicking or pressing the left mouse button
F9-Delete	Double-clicking or pressing the right mouse button

Table 18.1: Key Functions under Paintbrush

The Elements of Paintbrush

Let's look at the various parts of the Paintbrush application window.
You can see the window in Figure 18.1.

Toolbox

The *Toolbox* contains tools for creating drawings. You can draw
lines, rectangles or circles, erase, spray-paint, and do much more.
The current, or selected, function is highlighted.

*Drawing
cursor*

The drawing cursor marks the actual cursor position. It changes
shape to represent the tool you're using. When you press the mouse
button, you can begin drawing lines, rectangles, or perform whatever function the tool you've chosen is intended for.

*Drawing
area*

The drawing area's size varies depending on the graphics card and
how much memory is available. Specify the size of the drawing area
with the Image Attributes option on the Options menu.

*Linesize
box*

Select a line width from the *Linesize box* when you draw lines or
geometric figures.

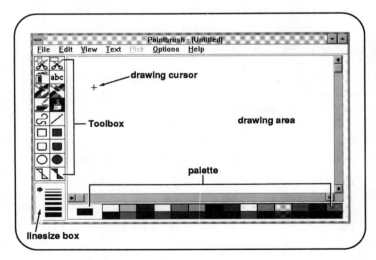

Figure 18.1: The elements of Paintbrush

The *Palette* shows you which colors are available by default. You can use the colors to draw or to fill in an area.

Palette

If you are working with the keyboard, use the Tab key to switch between the Toolbox, Linesize box, Palette, and drawing area. Use the arrow keys to reposition the pointer, and select a new feature by pressing the Insert key. Working with the mouse gives you free access to all of these resources.

Defining the Window Size

Paintbrush establishes a standard size for all documents. The standard size is determined by the graphics card and the graphic mode being used (VGA, SuperVGA, 8514/A, etc.). If you want to change the standard size, select Image Attributes on the Options pull-down menu. You will see the dialog box shown in Figure 18.2.

Changing the size of the document

Here you can determine, among other things, the size of a standard document in inches, centimeters, or pels (pixels). The values you choose will apply to the current document. By pressing the Default command button, you can make the values you choose the new standard size for all documents. You can also tell Paintbrush whether you want to draw in color or in black and white only.

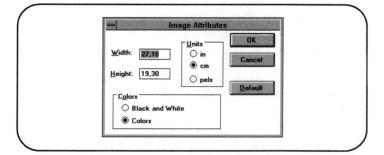

Figure 18.2: Image attributes define the document size

Moving within the Document

Moving around the document with the mouse is self-explanatory. Use the scroll bars to move to different parts of the picture. The key-combinations shown in Table 18.3 are also available for moving around the document.

Keys for moving around documents

Key	Moves To
Home	Top of the drawing area
End	Bottom of the drawing area
PgUp	One screen-page up
PgDn	One screen-page down
Shift-↑	Up a line
Shift-↓	Down a line
Shift-→	Right a space
Shift-←	Left a space
Shift-Home	Left side of the document
Shift-End	Right side of the document
Shift-PgUp	One screen to the left
Shift-PgDn	One screen to the right

Table 18.3: Key Functions for Moving Around a Document

Zooming in and out

You can enlarge or reduce a section of the document to examine it in detail or to see what it looks like in its entirety. These features are available through the Zoom In and Zoom Out options on the View pull-down menu.

- To see the entire picture on the screen, select the View Picture menu item on the View pull-down menu, or press Ctrl-P.

- To enlarge a section of the picture, press Ctrl-N or select Zoom In by moving the box that appears on the screen with the cursor keys or mouse. Next, press Insert or click the left button and select a section of the picture to zoom in on. Figure 18.3 shows an enlarged portion of a picture that has been "zoomed in on."

To zoom out, or reduce the size of a picture display, press Ctrl-O or select Zoom Out from the View menu.

Using the Clipboard

You can insert the contents of the Clipboard into a Paintbrush document by pressing Ctrl-V or by selecting the Paste item on the Edit menu. The contents of the Clipboard will appear in the upper-left corner of the window. From there, you can place the picture anywhere you want in the window.

Inserting Clipboard contents

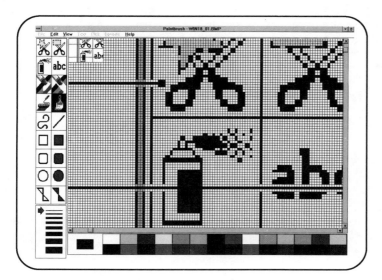

Figure 18.3: Paintbrush can zoom in on sections of a picture.

Editing Colors

You can modify the colors provided to you in the Palette. Select Edit Colors from the Options pull-down menu. Now you can create countless colors and shades of colors.

Printing a Drawing

If you want to print a drawing, select Print from the File menu. You can specify how many copies to print, whether to print a section or the whole drawing, and in what scale to print the drawing.

Leaving Paintbrush

To leave Paintbrush, select Exit from the File menu. Paintbrush will remind you if you have modified the current document. You will be given the opportunity to save it. The document will not be lost if you minimize Paintbrush to icon size.

Windows 3.1 Accessories

Besides feature-rich accessory applications such as Paintbrush and Write, each of which could have its own *Up & Running* book, Windows has always come with a set of fairly useful accessories. This Step briefly describes each of them.

Starting Accessories Applications

Each application is in the Accessories program group of the Program Manager. To start one of the accessories, open the Accessories group window and double-click on the appropriate icon. Below is a brief description of each application.

Terminal

Windows 3.1 comes with Terminal, a data communications program, as standard equipment. With Terminal, you can exchange data with other computers over telephone lines, for example.

In order to exchange data between two computers with Terminal, certain minimum requirements must be met. You need an open serial port and

Hardware requirements

- a modem with appropriate cable if the data is to be transferred over telephone lines; or
- A null-modem cable if the two computers are in one room and are to be connected directly.

The Clock

The system clock was one of the first applications available with Windows. In the first version of Windows, it demonstrated the program's multitasking capability: several windows could be opened with the clock appearing in each one.

In earlier versions of Windows, the window size of an application was a function of the system, but under Windows 3.1 you decide the clock's size and position. The clock also looks more modern (see Figure 19.1). You can also select a digital clock or suppress the date display.

The Cardfile

Organizing addresses

Cardfile is an electronic index card file for organizing addresses. With it, you can create individual cards according to your needs. For example, you could create address cards with the names, addresses and telephone numbers of your friends or business associates. Cardfile is shown in Figure 19.2.

Index line

The first line of the card is called the Index line of the file. Here you enter a keyword alphabetically by pressing F6 or by double-clicking on the Index line. Cardfile will use the keyword to sort the file alphabetically. The Index line has a special place value comparable to that of an index field in a database.

Adding a card

To add a new index card to a file, Press F7. A window will appear on the screen. Here you enter the contents of the Index line.

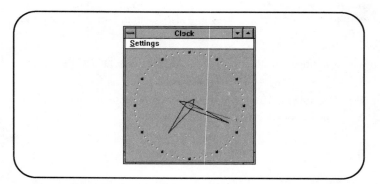

Figure 19.1: The system clock

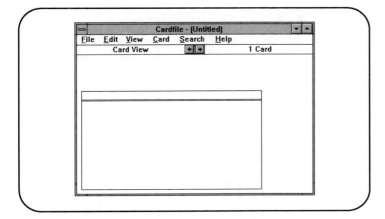

Figure 19.2: Use Cardfile for storing addresses.

Cardfile presents all entries in the form of index cards on the screen. You can also view the entries in list form. Select the form of presentation from the View menu.

Viewing Cards

You can bring a card to the foreground with the mouse. Select the Index line of the card to do this. If you want to use the keyboard, see Table 19.1 for the commands that apply.

Looking through the cards

Press	To View
PgUp	the previous card
PgDn	the next card
Ctrl-Home	the first card
Ctrl-End	the last card
↑	the previous card (in List mode)
↓	the next card (in List mode)

Table 19.1: Key Functions in Cardfile

Finding a card

If you want to find a specific card, press F4 and enter the Index line of the card. It will appear on the top of the stack.

Searching for Text

With the help of the Find function, you can search for text on a card. The Index line will remain excluded from the search. Cardfile stops at every entry that contains the search text. Press F3 to continue the search operation.

Merging Cardfile files

You can merge several card files. To do this, select the Merge menu item from the File menu and enter the name of the second Cardfile file. The cards will be merged and sorted alphabetically.

The Calendar

Windows 3.1 comes with an easy-to-use calendar. With the Calendar program, you can schedule appointments, for example.

After you start the Calendar program, you see a calendar pad of the current day, as shown in Figure 19.3. The day is divided into hours

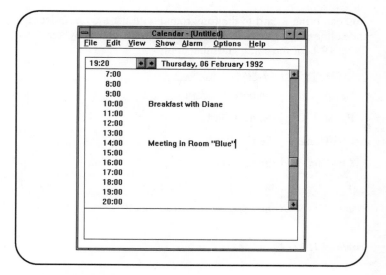

Figure 19.3: A daily schedule in the Calendar

from 7 AM to 8 PM. You can attach a brief note to each of the times listed.

The Calendar program offers two views, one for individual days and one for the month. You can switch between the two display modes by pressing F8 and F9 or by way of the View menu. You can select a day in the Month view by double-clicking or by pressing Enter. The day's hourly schedule will be displayed automatically.

Monthly or daily view

You can set an alarm and have it go off on any given day or time. To do this, move the cursor to the time when you want the alarm to go off and press F5. A small icon will appear in the left border to represent the alarm function. With the Controls menu item on the Alarm menu, you can define how many minutes before the appointment the alarm should go off. You can also turn off the audible alarm if you so prefer.

The Alarm

By default, the Calendar program divides the day into hourly intervals. You can change to 15 or 30 minute intervals with the Day Settings item on the Options menu. You can also specify whether to use a 12- or 24-hour format and define how the time intervals appear on the calendar pad (which is not to imply that you can't define an appointment for an earlier time).

Changing the time format

The Notepad

The Notepad, shown in Figure 19.4, is a text editor for editing text files. It is similar to EDIT, the DOS text editor.

Text editor

You can read nearly any text file into the Notepad, but it normally works with text files having the file extension .TXT. The Notepad does not wrap lines of text to the next line. However, if you switch on the Word Wrap option on the Edit menu, the Notepad will wrap words to the next line. This way, no information is hidden because it runs off the screen.

Search for text

The Notepad allows you to search for strings of characters in a text file. To do this, choose the Search menu item and enter the character string that you want to find. If case is relevant, make sure the Match

Searching for text

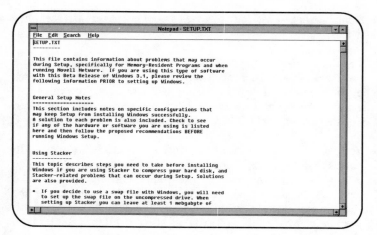

Figure 19.4: The Notepad, a text editor

Case option is activated. You can search upward or downward through a file. The Notepad will highlight character strings when it finds them. Press F3 to continue the search.

Time-Log

By placing the characters .LOG in the first line of any Notepad file, Notepad will automatically add the current time and date to the end of the file each time it is opened.

Calculator

The Calculator, shown in Figure 19.5, has been a part of Windows from the beginning. Use the Calculator as you would an ordinary pocket calculator. You can choose between the Standard and Scientific format from the View menu.

Scientific format

The scientific calculator is more powerful than the standard one. It can do conversions between decimal, hexadecimal, and binary values, for example. It also offers degree systems and many functions to choose from in scientific mode.

Use the standard calculator for simple chores.

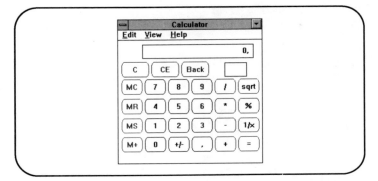

Figure 19.5: The Calculator

Step 20

Optimizing Windows 3.1

As long as you know Windows' procedures well and can set the system resources of your computer, you can optimize Windows. Unfortunately, you can't optimize Windows during the automatic installation procedure. To optimize the performance of Windows, you must configure Windows 3.1 manually.

Optimizing Windows means achieving the right configuration for the entire system. That is, you want to obtain an ideal balance of speed, maximum memory usage of RAM, and free memory capacity. The most important of the three is obtaining an optimal use of available main memory. That means altering the DOS configuration file (CONFIG.SYS).

The right configuration

Configuration for an 80286 Processor

On a PC with an 80286, you can operate Windows in Standard mode. To run in Standard mode, your computer needs at least 1 Mb main memory (640K base memory and 256K extended memory). If at least this much memory is available, Windows starts automatically in Standard mode.

Avoid using expanded memory with Windows. Windows operates better in Standard mode with extended memory. If you can configure your memory expansion, set up as little expanded memory as possible. The following settings should be in your CONFIG.SYS file:

- A command line for installing a device driver, such as HIMEM.SYS, which administers extended memory.

- If you want to access expanded memory, a device driver that handles expanded memory in your system, such as EMM.SYS.

- A FILES statement with at least 30 open files allowed (FILES=30).

Setting the CONFIG. SYS file for an 80286

- A BUFFERS command line. As a rule, you should set up about 20 buffers (BUFFERS=20). If you are working with SMARTDRV, the statement could also be BUFFERS=10.

- A command line that installs the hard-disk cache program SmartDrive (as long as there is sufficient memory).

- If you work in Standard mode with DOS applications and your computer is outfitted with an EGA card, the EGA.SYS device driver should also be loaded, like so:

```
device=c:\windows\ega.sys
```

Configuration for an 80386 Processor (or Higher)

Only computers with at least an 80386 processor can work in Enhanced mode, the most powerful operating mode. However, at least 2Mb of RAM are required to run in Enhanced mode.

Require-
ments

At startup, Windows checks whether your system meets the requirements for operating in Enhanced mode. If, for instance, no HIMEM driver is installed, Windows will not start in Enhanced mode, independent of available extended memory. Therefore, you need the following settings in your CONFIG.SYS file:

Setting the
CONGIF.
SYS file for
an 80386

- A command line for installing a device driver, such as HIMEM.SYS, which administers extended memory.

- If you want to access expanded memory, a device driver that handles expanded memory in your system, such as EMM386.SYS. In any case, you should dedicate as little memory as possible to expanded memory.

- A FILES statement with at least 30 open files allowed (FILES=30).

- A BUFFERS command line. As a rule, you should set up about 20 buffers (BUFFERS=20). If you are working with SMARTDRV, the statement could also be BUFFERS=10.

- A command line that installs the hard-disk cache program SmartDrive (as long as there is sufficient memory).

- If you work in Standard mode with DOS applications and your computer is outfitted with an EGA card, the EGA.SYS device driver should also be loaded, like so:

```
device=c:\windows\ega.sys
```

Optimizing Hard Disk Speed

Windows 3.1 frequently accesses the hard disk found in the system, so a drive with the quickest possible access time is desirable. Of course, you can't change the technical capabilities of your hard disk, but you can speed up its performance. To optimize hard disk speed, observe the following principles:

- Erase unnecessary directories and files. Unused Windows components can be removed using the new features of the SETUP program, which are described in Step 16.

  Cleaning up the disk

- Erase all lost clusters using the DOS CHKDSK/F command or a comparable utility, such as Norton's SpeedDisk. Lost clusters are found on nearly every hard disk.

- Defragment all files and optimize the logical structure. You can do this with optimization programs such as Norton's SpeedDisk.

  Remove fragmentation

- Use CHKDSK/F or SpeedDisk only when Windows is not running. Never run CHDSK/F or SpeedDisk from Windows. You must call these programs from the DOS prompt. If you don't, you are likely to lose data.

Windows Swap Files

In Enhanced mode, you can put additional memory at the disposal of Windows applications by setting up a swap file. This additional memory—it expands the computer's actual memory (RAM)—is called *virtual memory*. Windows applications do not distinguish between real and virtual memory. Think of virtual memory as a complement to the memory that is actually available.

Virtual memory

Before you can access virtual memory, you must set up a swap file. Windows 3.1 recognizes two types of swap files, temporary and permanent.

Permanent swap file

You, the user, can set up a *permanent* swap file. Permanent swap files are not erased when you exit Windows—they are always available. You specify the size of the swap file yourself. You can alter its size at any time.

Because it consists of logically contiguous blocks on the hard disk, a permanent swap file is by nature quicker than a temporary one.

Temporary swap file

Windows sets up a temporary swap file automatically when Enhanced mode is being used and it can't find a permanent swap file. How big a temporary swap file is depends on the amount of free space available on your hard disk. Temporary swap files are set up when you start Windows and erased when you exit the program.

Setting Virtual Memory

If you are working in Enhanced mode, set up a permanent swap file. To do so, procede as follows:

Setting up a permanent swap file

1. Compress your hard disk with a utility designed for that purpose, such as SpeedDisk.

2. To be safe, close all unrequired applications.

3. Start 386 Enhanced from the Control Panel.

4. Click the Virtual Memory control button. The current settings will be displayed.

5. Specify the size of the swap file with the Change option. You can also specify whether to install a permanent or temporary swap file and on which hard disk drive to install it. Use a drive that still has sufficient free space.

6. Confirm by clicking on OK. Confirm the dialog box asking you to verify your decision.

You must start Windows again to make your settings take effect. Either do this immediately or later on.

Changing the Size of a Swap File

Of course, you can change the size or type of swap file used in Enhanced mode. To do so, procede as follows:

1. Start 386 Enhanced from the Control Panel.

2. Click the Virtual Memory control button. The current settings will be displayed.

3. Click the Change command button and specify the size and type of swap file. Make the desired modifications.

4. Confirm by clicking on OK. Confirm the dialog box asking you to verify your decision.

To make your settings take effect, you must start Windows again. You can to do this immediately or later on.

Deleting a Swap File

To remove a permanent swap file after you've installed it (which you might do to make more room on your hard disk, for instance) follow the steps described above. Next, under Type, select

- None if you want to avoid using swap files altogether

- Temporary if you would rather work with a temporary swap file than a permanent one. You would select Temporary, for example, if you knew that the disk space required for the temporary file would be freed up once you left Windows.

Using SmartDrive

SmartDrive is a hard-disk cache program that makes it easier for the system to access the hard disk (the file name is SMARTDRV.EXE).

Whenever a sector is read or written to, SmartDrive copies it to a separate memory cache. The larger the memory cache allocated to SmartDrive, the more sectors it can store. SmartDrive notes not only the contents of the sector, but also its "name"—that is, its sector number.

If your system requests a sector that has been copied to the memory cache, SmartDrive just goes to the memory cache in RAM—it doesn't have to access the hard disk. Because accessing RAM is incomparably faster than accessing the fastest hard disk, a considerable improvement in operating speed can be achieved with SmartDrive.

Advantages
of
SmartDrive

SmartDrive offers numerous advantages:

- SmartDrive is automatically installed during the installation if enough memory is available.

- SmartDrive is easy to install.

- SmartDrive improves the operating speed of your system considerably.

The only disadvantage of using SmartDrive is that it reduces the amount of available memory.

Under Windows 3.1, SmartDrive is no longer a device driver. It is an ordinary DOS command, and you should integrate it into your AUTOEXEC.BAT file.

Moreover, SmartDrive has noticeably improved. For example, it now supports floppy-disk drives as well. Now you can also decide which disk drives SmartDrive should watch over and which drives it should not. Above all, SmartDrive now stores and optimizes on write-accesses.

Installing SmartDrive

You install SmartDrive in the AUTOEXEC.BAT file of DOS. The installing entry is made automatically during the installation procedure and should look something like this:

```
c:\windows\smartdrv
```

For the memory cache, SMARTDRV uses extended memory by default. The size of the cache memory is determined automatically and depends on the size of the available working memory (RAM).

The memory allocated for SMARTDRV will not always be used. Windows looks to SMARTDRV only when it has memory problems. Normally, SMARTDRV frees up part of the memory reserved for the cache and places it temporarily at the disposal of Windows. When Windows no longer needs the memory, SmartDrive again uses it.

SmartDrive has many options for influencing how it functions. You can see a description of the available options if you call SmartDrive with the Option /?, like so:

Options

```
smartdrv /?
```

Index

configuration and CONFIG.SYS
  file, 2
  optimizing, 133–135
  Setup program for, 5–9,
    107–111
  with upgrading, 5
context-sensitive help, 4
Control menus, 17, 19–21
  for dialog boxes, 26
  for File Manager, 49
  for group windows, 39–40
  items on, 31–33
  for Task Manager, 66
Control Panel
  for color, 99–100
  for Desktop, 101–103
  for Enhanced mode, 104–105
  for fonts, 89–90
  for international settings, 104
  for mouse, 101
  for multimedia, 94–97
  for printers, 104
  for sound, 105
copying
  to Clipboard, 83–84
  files, 56
  program icons, 43
corners, window, 19
country codes, 104
cursor blink rate, 103
custom colors, 99–100
Custom Setup, 3–5, 7–9

D

data communications
  program, 125

dates, 104, 125–126, 128–129
default command buttons, 29–30
default directory, 51–52
DEFAULT.PIF file, 75
deleting
  files, 56
  fonts, 89–90
  print files, 71
  program icons, 43
  swap files, 137
Desktop, 101–103
device contention, 105
device drivers
  for multimedia, 94–95
  with upgrading, 5
dialog boxes, 25–27
  command buttons in, 29–30
  using, 28–29
dimmed command buttons,
    26, 29
dimmed menu items, 33, 35
directories, 1
  displaying, 48–52, 54
  for PIFs, 74, 76
  for program items, 42
  selecting, 51–52
  for Windows, 4–5
Directory region, 50
directory tree, 48–52
disks. *See* hard disks
document windows, 15–16
DOS
  command prompt for, 61–63
  Setup program from, 111
DOS applications
  closing, 45
  exchanging data with, 78, 83

and operating modes, 11–12, 59
PIF files for, 7, 73–79
printing in, 70
dot-matrix printers, 91
double-clicking, 101
drag and drop feature, 56–57, 60
drawing, 119–124
drivers
  for multimedia, 94–95
  with upgrading, 5
drives, 1
  icons for, 50
  selecting, 50–51
  windows for, 52–54
Dynamic Data Exchange (DDE),
    81–83

E

Edit menus, 35
ellipses (...), 29, 35
embedding objects, 82, 84–85
EMM.SYS driver, 133–134
end marks, 113
ending tasks, 67
Enhanced mode, 11–13
  Control Panel for, 104–105
  PIFs for, 74, 77–78
  requirements for, 2
error messages, 25
events for Wave files, 96
exchanging data
  with Clipboard, 81–84
  with DDE, 81–83
  with DOS applications, 78, 83

with OLE, 82–86
with Paintbrush, 123
exiting
  File Manager, 57
  Paintbrush, 124
  PIF editor, 79
  Print Manager, 71
  Program Manager, 45
  Setup, 112
  Task Manager, 65
  Windows, 14
  Write, 118
Express Setup, 3–4
extensions, 1

F

File Manager
  directory tree with, 50–52
  drag and drop feature with,
      56–57
  drive windows with, 52–54
  exiting, 57
  manipulating files with, 56
  organization of, 48–50
  selecting files with, 54–55
  starting, 47–48
  starting applications with,
      59–60
File menus, 34–35
files, 1
  copying, moving, and
      deleting, 56
  displaying, 48–52, 54
  fragmented, 135

N

names
for files, 1, 75
for groups, 40
for PIFs, 74
networks
print queues for, 70
setting for, 108
non-Windows applications. *See*
DOS applications
Notepad program, 129–130
numeric fields, 26, 29

O

Object Linking and Embedding
(OLE), 82–86
operating modes, 11–14
Control Panel for, 104–105
for DOS applications, 11–12,
59
PIFs for, 74–78
requirements for, 2
optimizing
configurations for, 133–135
disk cache programs for,
137–139
hard disks, 135
swap files, 135–137
option buttons, 27–28
overlapping windows, 15, 68

P

page status area, 113
Paintbrush, 119–124
Palettes in Paintbrush, 121
parameters in PIFs, 76
pasting from Clipboard, 84, 123
paths, 1, 42
permanent swap files, 9, 136
PIFs (Program Information
Files), 7, 59, 73–79
ports, 7, 100
positioning. *See* moving
PostScript printers, 92
Print Manager, 69–71
printers
Control Panel for, 104
selecting, 6–7
printing
drawings, 124
files, 69–71
TrueType fonts for, 91–92
priorities
in PIFs, 77
in printing, 71
program groups. *See* groups
program icons, 37, 39, 41–43
Program Manager
creating and expanding groups
with, 40–43
elements of, 38–40
exiting, 45
and File Manager, 47–48
reducing to icon, 44

and standard groups, 37–38
starting applications with,
59–60
properties for program items,
41–43
pull-down menus
Control menu, 31–32
conventions for, 34–35
selecting items from, 32–34

Q

queues, printer, 69–71

R

Real mode, 11
repeat rate, key, 103
replacing
old versions, 4–5
Write text, 116–118
requirements, system, 2
restoring windows, 21

S

scheduling appointments,
128–129
scientific calculator, 130

screen, copying, 84
screen savers, 101–102
scroll bars, 19, 27–28
searching
for applications, 7, 9, 42, 60,
109–110
in Cardfile files, 128
for Notepad text, 129–130
for Write text, 116–118
selecting
active windows, 66–67
applications, 67
directories, 51–52
drives, 50–51
files, 54–55
menu items, 32–34
printers, 6–7
text, 115–116
serial ports, 7, 100
Setup program, 3–4
for configuration, 5–6, 107–111
for Custom Setup, 7–9
from DOS, 111
exiting, 112
for PIFs, 73
for printers, 6–7
shortcut keys
in dialog boxes, 28–29
for menus, 34
in PIFs, 78
for program items, 42
single-line list boxes, 27
size
of clock, 126